Albanian Spring

Ismail Kadare

ALBANIAN SPRING
The Anatomy of Tyranny

Translated from the French by
Emile Capouya

Saqi Books

British Library Cataloguing-in-Publication Data
A catalogue record for this book is available from the
British Library

ISBN 0 86356 253 1 (hb)
ISBN 0 86356 174 8 (pbk)

First published as
Printemps Albanais
by Librairie Arthème Fayard, Paris 1991
© Librairie Arthème Fayard 1991

English translation copyright © 1994, Emile Capouya

This edition first published 1995
Saqi Books
26 Westbourne Grove
London W2 5RH

Contents

Introduction   7

Part One. *A Chronicle*   11

Part Two. *Letters*   89

Part Three. *Hope*   115

Notes   183

Introduction

These are a writer's notes, and while the events mentioned here have nothing to do with literature directly, they can only be understood from the literary point of view. No other perspective will give a clear picture, just as a pair of eyeglasses picked up at random will rarely suit the eyes of the person who tries them on.

In periods of political tension of the sort commonly called 'parlous times,' a writer is often ordered to remake himself completely—to give up that which makes him a writer. He is tugged this way and that by contending factions. The totalitarian state, spouting catchwords like 'understanding our life and times' and 'identifying with the masses,' has insisted that the writer give up literature and turn himself into a reporter, so as to glorify 'reality'—that is to say, to glorify the ruling power. The opposition, for its part, has pursued the same goal, but in the opposite direction. The writers must abandon literature and draw up an indictment of the regime. From the left as from the right, in the East as in the West, the same thing is expected of the writer—that he deny his individuality and become someone else. That demand is couched in high-sounding phrases such as 'The times cry out for . . ., etc'. Or, more solemnly, it is spoken of as 'the historical imperative. . ., etc'.

In short, in the name of morality the writer is ordered to do something amoral. In the name of life the writer is called on to die. The fact is that in parlous times, many people cannot bear even the mention of literature. Literature is a provocation. People call it a luxury, one to be enjoyed in the future, in a more tranquil future. Yet, even assuming that this future will produce a climate more favourable to literature—which is far from certain—it is likely that we shall never live to see it.

Those who brandish the 'state of emergency' like a flag forget that the writer cannot be held hostage to any age, nor bend the knee to its laws simply because he lives in that age. Working outside the realm of temporal constraints, the writer enjoys a life in which time is eternal. He obeys one law only, that of Art, and if the laws of the period in which he happens to live do not agree with the supreme law of Art, the writer can turn his back on the times.

And, contrary to what is often thought, those parlous times when dictators rage suit literature quite well. Dictatorship and literature coexist in only one relation: they devour each other day and night. A writer is the natural enemy of dictatorship. At every instant, even when he thinks he is slumbering, he wars with dictatorship. That has been inscribed in his genetic code. Dictatorship and literature can only exist together as two wild beasts that have each other by the throat. Each has its own very different laws and taboos, and each is capable of wounding the other in different ways. The writer's wounds seem horrible because they come at once. But those the writer inflicts on dictatorship are like a time bomb, and they never heal. The writer follows a different calendar, as is suggested in my book *Invitation to the Writer's Studio.*[1]*

Far from weakening under the tyrant's fevered assault, the instinct that pits the writer against dictatorship is hardened and strengthened, much as an animal learns to resist attack. That may explain how the novel which launched the most ferocious attack on the dictatorship, *The Palace of Dreams*,[2] could be written and published in Albania in 1981, when that country was going through its most ugly and dangerous phase. In such times, the suggestion that the writer renounce literature amounts to taking away his shield in the heat of battle. Literature has been his origin, his fertile soil, his power, his magic gift. Without her, his enemy would slice him up like a green sprout.

---

* The author's notes appear as endnotes at the back of the text.

And so, the remarks that follow are the remarks a writer—and of a man who has been at some pains to remain a writer. A man whom literature has led to freedom—it was certainly not freedom that led him to literature. His advance may have been slow, but in a sense it has mirrored the pace of his countrymen. His people, in 1912, were the last to free themselves of the Turkish yoke, and, in 1990, they were the last to break free of Stalinism. Yet tardiness does not necessarily mean backwardness. During that slow advance, as if under an impenetrable shell, there was a ripening within, and the dawning of an inner light. In 1912, when the Albanians emerged from a night of five centuries, they were well prepared to enter upon a new life. Although the storm of World War had ravaged the young state, in 1924 Albania was nevertheless one of three or four genuinely democratic nations of Europe—until another tempest came to destroy it. In 1945 at Yalta, as if driven by fate, Albania was once more relegated to the East, to that part of the world from which she had severed herself with such difficulty.

Today, at century's end, the orphaned nation which has long borne a heavy cross is knocking at the gates of Europe—at the gates of her mother, who has always treated her as a stepchild, and who, despite her claims of Christian charity, has not been kind to the waif.

PART ONE

A Chronicle

1

The telephone rang late in the afternoon. The caller was a member of the President's Cabinet. 'There's some material here for you. They'll deliver it right away.' I knew that in official jargon many things might be described as 'material': an invitation, a question, an order, a birthday card, a notice, a letter. This last was what came to mind at once.

And, in fact, a quarter of an hour later, I held in my hand an envelope containing a letter from the President. Before opening it, I said to my wife, 'This letter will do me no good.' She didn't answer. My sense of foreboding was not unfounded.

Three weeks earlier I had sent a long letter to the President in which I raised some delicate and thorny issues. The letter was written in such a way as to require no answer. And, to tell the truth, I not only expected no answer, but I secretly hoped I might never get one.

But day after day in the two weeks following the dispatch of my letter, I had been watching its effects. In spite of a number of disappointments, it seemed to me that those effects were quite extraordinary: an immediate end to the activities of two sadists in the Sigurimi;** the adoption by the Assembly of a bill authorizing passports for foreign travel; the abrupt resignation of the President of the Supreme Court, whom I had denounced most severely; the warm welcome extended to Pérez de Cuellar and the promise that it symbolized; the feelings of relief and sympathy that prevailed everywhere.

** The Albanian secret police.

Now that the unwelcome envelope had come, I knew that the spell had been broken. When I opened it and read the letter, I saw that my presentiment had not misled me. The letter was profoundly disheartening. My wife, as if wanting to be innocent of the business a little longer, had prepared a cup of coffee for me, and she seemed quite cast down when she came into my study. She found me doing something that, as she told me later, had seemed to her at once incomprehensible and terrifying. She asked, 'Have you read it? What on earth are you doing?'

I could feel that my lips had curled into a grimace.

'I'm counting the number of times he uses the word "Party" in his letter. He reproaches me for not having mentioned it once in mine.'

'Well? Then you mean . . .'

I nodded. The letter was disastrous. It ruled out hope. It meant nothing but desolation.

I drank my coffee slowly, as if at a funeral. Then I suggested that we go outdoors. In the street we said to one another, almost in unison, 'It's hopeless. We must leave this country.'

That day was the twenty-fifth of May, 1990. The brief Albanian spring, more shy than any other, had come to an end.

2

That kind of spring generally takes root in winter.[1]

It was in December of 1989. My wife and I were on our way home after a trip to Sweden. Before returning to Tirana we wanted to spend a few days in Paris.

To give an impression of the turbulent events shaking Europe at the time, there is no better example than our arrival by aeroplane. Every event needs a symbol if it is to leave a trace in our memory. In this case, everything you might have read in the newspapers or heard on television resembled, point by point in our eyes, the disordered motion of the scudding clouds, the beads of mist scattering across the wings of the aircraft, the threatening gleam of distant lightning.

The crystalline Swedish December was now far away, and beneath us the dark continent unrolled, full of its distress. When we touched down again it seemed that the frame of the aeroplane transmitted its own fevered shaking to the earth.

But what awaited us in Paris shook us even more. The Romanian uprising had begun. In our friends' apartment in Neuilly we watched the drama unfold hour by hour. It was the first time we'd come to Paris without the slightest desire to be outdoors or to see anyone we knew. The news came to us every half-hour, sometimes more frequently, and we sat anchored in front of the television screen as never before in our lives. Ceauçescu's rally. The baleful whistling of the crowd. Their astonishment. Shots fired in the gloom. Chaos. Then Ceauçescu's body sprawled on the ground, the knot of his red necktie like a bloodstain. The wall of the abandoned barracks. Everything repeated endlessly as in a bad dream. No, we were no longer in Paris.

We were in a hybrid place, a kind of Buchaparis that wanted to call itself Tirana. No, this could never happen in Tirana. Nothing like this. Never.

What can we do for Albania? That was the question put to me while I was dining in Stockholm with my friend Pierre Schory, Vice-Minister of Foreign Affairs in Sweden. 'What can you do? Something that might convince Albania not to fear democracy,' was my answer. I was not unaware that this would be a task of some difficulty, but I knew, too, that the most difficult things are the things we dream of most.

It was a cold day when we arrived in Tirana. From the moment our youngest daughter met us at the airport and all through the long drive home, she told us the news. There was unrest everywhere; someone had thrown a bomb at the statue of Stalin on the avenue, another bomb had been thrown at the Flora bookshop[*] next to our apartment building. Everyone knew what was happening in Romania.

From both sides of the road as we drove I was assailed by the familiar display of poverty, and by the pain I feel each time I return from abroad. My empty heart filled with sorrow.

---

[*] The classics of Marxism-Leninism and the works of Enver Hoxha were sold there.

3

It was one of the most sullen winters that Albania has ever known. Distress, raw nerves, exasperation were everywhere. Nevertheless, there were reports of a silent demonstration in Shkodra. The crowd had attempted to bring down the statue of Stalin. It was said that they managed to get a rope around the statue's neck, but the *sampists** and the police intervened. Many arrests were made that night. Most of those arrested were taken away in ambulances so as not to attract attention. There were several accounts of events that night, but no one had accurate information until two or three days later. People had indeed assembled in the town square in front of the bust of Stalin, and they had indeed brought a rope, but they had not succeeded in putting the rope around the statue's neck. The confrontation between the crowd and the police lasted for some time. In the end the demonstrators were dispersed, not sure whether they had gained or lost a point.

February came, and was even more gloomy than January. People said that something like the demonstration in Shkodra would happen in Tirana, but no one knew when or how. The government was placed on constant alert, and people's moods seemed to change from hour to hour.

Clouds covered the city as never before. Then someone announced the date of the demonstration, and even the place and time: Skanderberg Square, Sunday, at six o'clock in the evening. It was incomprehensible, something out of Kafka. For one thing, no one

---

* The riot squad.

17

knew who had made the decision. Even more puzzling was the choice of time and place. At that hour Skanderberg Square is always jammed with people. How could you tell the demonstrators from the usual crowd of people out for an evening walk, and how could you distinguish between these two groups and the members of the Sigurimi, who would certainly be there in the hundreds?

As if that weren't odd enough, there was to be a concert just at six, performed by a foreign ensemble, at the Opera, whose doors open onto the square. Traditionally, the diplomatic corps attends such performances. From the Sigurimi's point of view, it was clear that a demonstration would take place only with the complicity of foreign diplomats—especially since, for days, Yugoslav television had been reporting that two hundred journalists were massed on the Albanian-Yugoslav border in anticipation of an 'extraordinary event'.

In Tirana there was only one topic of conversation: six o'clock, Sunday, in the square. People were waiting impatiently, fearfully, with curiosity, with hope. The government's zeal in trying to avoid the worst that might happen invited even more speculation about what people were already referring to as a riotous mob, a demonstration, a hostile uprising, and even a stroll in the square. Units of the Front[*] were patrolling from door to door, saying, 'Don't go to the square tonight at six. See to it that the young people in particular do not go there.'

Drama and comedy were confounded. My mother warned my sister: 'Someone from the Front came to say that no one may go out, because the enemy has seized Skanderberg Square.' The fever was everywhere.

At five o'clock our daughter Besiana, a high-school girl, came to my study and said, 'Daddy, I'd like to go out at six o'clock with a friend.' 'Do as you like,' I said. Then she told my wife, who gave the same reply. Besiana dashed about the house, very excited, but we pretended not to notice. To compound our troubled thoughts, we each had a strange feeling that we were trying to dispel.

---

[*] A political group controlled by the Communist Party.

Besiana came back to my study where my wife and I were drinking coffee. This time her question was quite unexpected. 'Should I dress up or should I . . .?'

We told her to wear her everyday things. Just before six her friend came for her. Then six o'clock struck. Five past six. The square was only a hundred yards from our building, but we heard nothing.

At twenty past six Elena and I went out. At first sight, the square, as usual, was thronged with people. They were jammed together so that at a distance it was hard to make out the demonstrators, the Sigurimi agents, the *sampists,* the Party Committee militants, and the faithful veterans excited about the prospect of launching yet another surprise attack for the 'Cause'. Everything was mixed up, part reality, part dream. One person's guess was as good as another's, and each might have asked his neighbour, 'Who are you? Under what flag do you serve? Is it a face or a mast that you present to me? And what role do you play in this drama?'

You could feel the tension from far off. As we reached the square a calm voice rose powerfully from among a group of young people: 'Too late!' Farther away, another voice: 'Look at this nation. See how frightened they are!' Other calls rang out from other groups, but all were sober, serious, earnest. Sigurimi agents, Party militants, informers—they all had slipped into the crowd. Everyone knew that hidden cameras were taking photographs from vehicles that looked like ambulances. But no one cared. Fear rose like a vapour from the dark earth, but it was all right. In this demonstration, which sometimes resembled a promenade, there was something captivating, like first love or one's first dance. There was a holiday atmosphere, yet mixed with it a certain reserve, a certain gravity, and one would not have been surprised to hear the language of long ago, of the time when there were cathedrals in Albania. There was a glint in the young people's eyes—not a trace of hysteria or violence—and in my mind, clearer than ever, the thought grew, 'God be praised, things will not happen here as they happened in Romania!'

When I was home again I couldn't help repeating over and over, 'Too late.' I knew people expected more of me, but my friends had insisted that I not go out under any circumstances on that Sunday at six o'clock. The Sigurimi had been keeping me under watch for some time, threats had been directed at me from both the left and the right, and my presence at the demonstration might have seemed a heaven-sent occasion to settle my account. An incident, a provocation plotted in advance and carried out, there, on the square. They would announce, 'The writer was killed by enemies of the people at the very moment when, with other militants, he was hurrying to defend the gains of the revolution.'

To make things worse, my opponents were blinded by panic. For them too, it was all new; with their nerves at fever pitch, they were ready for anything.

Very soon it was clear that events were coming to pass just as one might have expected. In the days that followed, the Sigurimi tried to persuade the government that a group of intellectuals in league with Western powers had organized the demonstration. A list was prepared (naturally, my name and those of my friends were high on the list), embracing a hundred and fifty people who were to be arrested or liquidated. The ghost of Vaclav Havel had haunted me for some time, but for the moment the Sigurimi seemed content to keep me under surveillance day and night.

4

February was indeed darker than January. It usually is the worst month of winter in Tirana. The Albanians have several sayings to describe this month, and, as far as I know, Albanian is the only European language in which it is called, with a sense of disdain, 'short'.* Indeed, sandwiched between a cold but noble January and a youthful March, February is bound to be a month of gloom.

Had there really been more deaths than usual that month, or was it just an impression arising from the fact that people were attending funerals, and were able, at those times, to hear more news than at any other time or place? Even in the old days people lowered their voices at funerals. It seems that the presence of death made their speech more precise, more reliable, discarding the pleasantries and banalities of everyday conversation. One can imagine the things that were said at those ceremonies in February 1990. Unbelievable predictions. Hope, lost hope, despair, hope renewed. There would be a softening of government policy. Retaliatory measures would be taken. There would be an extraordinary session of the Party. All those arrested for 'Sunday at six' would be freed. Ramiz Alia had said, 'Enough!'— although some people took this positively and others took it as a bad omen. Still others said there would be another demonstration. That's why they were hunting for the leaders. A group of prominent intellectuals had led the demonstration. They've destabilized Ramiz Alia. Etc.

Not all the speculation was unfounded. Each day brought new

---

* In Albanian, *shkurt.*

fluctuations on the part of the regime. Orders were issued—contradictory orders. One day the police were arrogant, armed with rubber truncheons. The next, they hung their heads, and had no truncheons. Another day and the cycle would begin again.

Everyone was caught as if in a whirlwind. To an outsider, it might have looked like madness. Given a chance, people would try to escape, if only in part. They asked their friends to dinner, they went to dances, pretending to live a normal life. But at the most unexpected times, when glasses were clinking, dancing partners were kissing, or flirtatious gestures were made, the question would suddenly burst forth: 'What is going to happen?'

That question led me to ask for an interview with the President. On 3 February at eleven o'clock I put in a request to his office, emphasizing that there was no special urgency, the President could see me at his convenience.

An hour later his secretary telephoned me: 'Comrade Ramiz would like to speak with you.'

On the telephone the President's voice was as casual as it had been in our earlier conversations. 'You've asked to see me? It would be a pleasure. You could come right now, but at half past twelve I must meet with two ambassadors.'

'Comrade Ramiz, as I told your secretary, it's not urgent.'

'Fine. As it happens I was hoping to see you. Shall we say tomorrow, then? We can set a time right now. Say, one o'clock. Is that all right with you?'

'As you please.'

I had known the President for a long time, but I was still susceptible to his courteous manner. It was not just a question of good breeding and etiquette. That kind of civility was the sign of a desire for dialogue. It put you at ease so that you could speak of all sorts of things—in fact, it encouraged you to do just that. I was grateful to him for it. Even at this moment, as I write these lines in France, setting aside all the things that have happened since, I still feel grateful to him. Just as dictatorship draws strength from many sources, visible and invisible, so too does liberty. A movement, a gesture, an exchange of ideas at the opportune time, can be indispensable in giving one the courage to go forward. That is why there is no reason to withhold gratitude from those who were once deserving, even if only for a short while, and even if they acted quite differently later on.

I knew the President well, not only because I had often had business with him in the quarter century that he served as Director of Propaganda and Culture, but also because of some unusual circumstances. We had two friends in common who had fallen into misfortune. Despite the fact that they were far away—one in semi-detention and the other in prison—they kept us bound to each other as if by a band of crepe. That tie, linking us to parties now faded into shadow, worked upon us with a special force. Under totalitarian regimes, it often happens that the condemnation of friends or acquaintances can bring darkness upon an entire circle of people. Friendship grows cold, people turn away from one another; they try to forget the dinners at which they once laughed and chatted together, perhaps because they believe that, just maybe, they can elude the danger which has threatened them for so long. For careerists and government functionaries, this kind of conduct is ten times as prevalent.

If nothing like that ever happened between Ramiz Alia and myself, the credit should be his, since he was the one most at risk. T. Lubonja,[2] one of the most gifted and intelligent people I have ever known, one of my two or three closest friends and Ramiz Alia's closest friend, is now languishing in the dungeon to which he was sentenced for fifteen years—yet even he never cast a shadow between us. On the contrary, Ramiz Alia's goodwill, and the esteem in which he held me—to which he alluded in his last letter*—were redoubled. I always regarded that goodwill as having a significance which extended beyond me personally. I thought of it as a kind of sadness about what might have been, a sense of longing, and a kind of loyalty to something that was gone, and hope, hope that good

---

* See the letters reprinted in Part Two of this book.

things might be hidden just beyond the horizon. And all this assumed an even greater significance because of my old friendship with Lubonja, particularly since it was well known that he held me in high regard. It was so well known, in fact, that I'd hear little recriminations here and there: It just goes to show, the two of them are a pair; in the old days they belonged to the same group; That's all right, our turn will come. The Party never forgets . . .

It seemed to me that because I was quick to fly off the handle—and just as quick to cool down—I had never really been angry with him. There certainly had been many occasions on which our relations might have turned sour. One of the most painful of these took place in 1975, in the very same office in which I was now going to meet him. His criticisms of me as author of a poem entitled *The Red Pashas*[3] were so violent (and spoken in the presence of a score of officials who took notes in deadly silence) that I interrupted him, and asked, 'If I understand you correctly, you think I am an enemy of this country?'

'That's for you to tell us,' he replied.

'Well, I'll tell you right now. I am not an enemy!'

(An hour later, when I was telling my wife what happened, I confessed that, while I was listening to his indictment, my eyes turned from time to time to the window, and I thought that it would be easier to throw myself out of it than to bear this horror.)

People who were at that meeting told me later that now, after the passing of time, they felt they had suffered a hallucination. It must certainly have been the most excoriating accusation ever levelled at an individual in my country. In the course of that meeting, it was not insignificant that Ramiz Alia uttered these words: 'I wonder if you understand what friendship means to me. I have always believed that friendship is at the centre of the Party's principles.' (At that time Lubonja had already spent two years in prison.) Even though his first sentence was couched as a question, I did not answer.

Things between us were strained once again in 1982, at a time when everyone knew that Alia would succeed Enver Hoxha, and that for all intents and purposes he was the leader of the country. On that occasion it was my novel, *The Palace of Dreams*, that furnished the pretext. Except for saying, 'I quite understand the criticisms expressed here for the benefit of literature,' I did not offer any self-criticism. And this was at the plenary meeting of the Writers' Union, in the presence of half the members of the Politburo, with the future President standing before them.

After that our relations went on as if nothing had happened. To tell the truth, I must have caused him a good deal of annoyance because half my books had run into trouble when they were published, and since he was in charge of propaganda, he was always the one blamed.

Then, too, I was not the only one for whom it would have been graceless to hold a grudge against him. I've spoken to other people who had had similar experiences with him. Perhaps that is why, in the spring of 1990, Ramiz Alia was admired by most Albanians—so much so that many placed their hopes on him—even some of those who were in prison.

5

It was one o'clock when I entered his office. I had prepared all morning for our meeting, and I felt no apprehension, no hesitation about any issue that might arise. I told him I had come to talk about everything, straightforwardly, and he replied that that was exactly what he expected of me. I knew very well that conversations in his office were recorded, but that didn't trouble me. On the contrary, I was pleased that there would be a record of what we said.

I spoke first of the difficulties confronting the Albanian nation, both inside Albania and in Kosovo, since those troubles—and those alone—called for all our intelligence and all our fervour. We also talked about events in Eastern Europe, about the situation in Romania, and about the two possible solutions for avoiding catastrophe in Albania: one, a crackdown, the choice favoured by conservatives; the other, democracy. When I emphasized that I believed he himself favoured democracy, he nodded. But to bring democracy, I continued, we had a long row to hoe, for certain things that had been thought excusable had now become intolerable. Then I got to the heart of the problem—the violation of human rights in Albania. I knew he had been incensed when I raised the question six months earlier in a review of *The Knives*, a novel by N. Tozaj, but that didn't trouble me at all. I had railed against him at the time, and I'm sure that it had been reported to him. But this kind of thing had been going on for nearly twenty years, and it hadn't destroyed our relations. I told him that, in Albania, we must rid ourselves once and for all of our idiotic conception of human rights—we must stop thinking in terms of the right to shelter, the right to work and the right to be protected by society, and must begin taking account of the violation of laws, of police violence, imprisonment, and dictatorship.

He listened for half an hour before interrupting, and then he spoke very calmly.

'But surely economic and social rights are features of human rights.'

'Of course they are, but they don't make sense if basic human rights are not protected—that is the dark side of the problem.'

I went on speaking to that issue, since I was only too aware that Albanian propaganda, with help from certain pseudo-philosophers and pseudo-academics, had for years pushed the idea that human rights violations could not be tied to the state, that they were the result of social problems, and must be treated differently in different countries.

I told him how two months earlier in Paris, during a meeting of the Academy of Moral and Political Science, which I was attending for the first time, the red flush of shame had risen to my ears, for the most important document presented addressed ways in which various dictatorships strove to justify oppression. Luckily the speaker had not mentioned Albania, I told him, but other dictatorships were specifically mentioned and they employed the same kinds of justification that we did.

He listened to me attentively and, following his cue, I said, 'The civilized world today has only one conception of human rights, which is to say that those rights are universal, and they cannot be parcelled out at the whim of individual nations. To say that human rights are not being violated in Albania is nonsense,' I continued. 'One had only to ask a simple question: Those ministers of the interior, condemned one after the other as criminals—what had they done? Everyone knows that their primary occupation was violating human rights from morning to night.'

He listened. Then, blushing, he nodded. 'You're right,' he said. 'The rights of man are being violated in Albania.'

That was the first time I had heard an admission like that, particularly from the Head of State.

Feeling encouraged, I spoke of the political prisoners. Albania had met all the conditions necessary for transforming itself into a truly democratic regime. Unlike other Balkan or Mediterranean peoples, the Albanians showed no propensity for anarchy. They respect the law no matter how severe or stupid (a legacy of their ancient Code). Let's say, to be brief, that in this matter they resemble the Germans, so that the process of democratization would not necessarily bring disorder or misunderstanding, as it had in some other countries. Albania might, for example, become a country with no political prisoners.

Here he interrupted and dwelt on the matter for some time. 'But,' he objected, 'what about our enemies, those who want to seize power by force? Are we to leave them at liberty?'

I answered that those who would attempt to seize power illegally do not constitute a political opposition, but rather are terrorists, and would be outlawed in any country.

We kept to that topic and he gave me a rough figure for the people imprisoned in Albania—a little less than five thousand, but he did not specify whether or not that number included political prisoners.

At that point in the discussion I took it upon myself to say, 'Tell me frankly, what objection is there to setting them all free? You know very well that most of them are innocent—like Lubonja, whom you finally released just recently. You also know that most of them pose no danger to the state, and that freeing them could bring enormous benefit to our country—even if some were to engage in "hostile activities". Any negative repercussions would be negligible compared to the benefits.'

I am sure that in his heart he agreed with me. He knew that incarcerating them was pointless. It was not the people he was afraid of, but something else. He was afraid of violating a taboo. A communist state is inconceivable without political prisoners—just as a house is inconceivable with neither foundation nor roof. We were talking about the very nature of dictatorship.

Nevertheless his objections were weak, and I felt I had achieved a qualified success.

In the following onslaught of ideas, still regarding matters of foreign policy, I broached another subject, although scarcely knowing why—perhaps I was eager for a more complete success, or possibly I just wanted to change the subject. In any case it was one of the most important headings in my notes, which I had written down as 'Cows!' I put the argument this way: 'Despite the claims of official propaganda, Albania is not a poor country, and the Albanians could and should be living much better. Albania is in every respect richer than Greece; generally speaking, in the past Albanians enjoyed a markedly higher standard of living than the Greeks. They ate better (in the southern part of the country, people remember Greek caravans that came to Albania to look for food), and their houses, except in some parts of the plain, were large and solidly built. More and more frequently people ask, "Why aren't we living better today? What has brought this about? What obstacle is in our way?"

'People everywhere are making a terrible accusation: it's that someone *doesn't want* them to live better, that someone believes that the people, more easily dominated, must be kept in misery.'

He interrupted, 'Who could possibly think such a thing?', but his tone was far from assured.

Because there had been no other explanation, I told him, the people had a right to supply that one. The government can mislead them with incessant propaganda about the worldwide economic crisis, credit swindles, the price of oil, low yields on investment, bureaucracy, liberalism, etc. But there comes a time when they can no longer be fooled. And that is where the awful question lies. Everyone knows that if we were to give cows and other livestock to the peasants, it would immediately result in their improved well-being. Cows are not subject to the international monetary system, nor to the price of oil, nor to American interests in the Gulf, nor even to the technological conversion of factories in Tirana, etc. What stands in the way of enacting such a measure? Marxist-Leninist doctrine? Lenin's thesis that smallholdings lead little by little to capitalism? In other words, socialism?

There were charlatans in the Central Committee who, on the

pretext of not wanting to tarnish the brilliance of Marxist principles, were prepared to let the Albanian people die of hunger. (Ramiz Alia himself had repeated an unhappy coinage of Enver Hoxha in a speech less than two years earlier: 'The Albanians shall eat grass rather than give up the defence of Marxism-Leninism'—but I didn't remind him of it.) Every now and then members of the regime would say, without compunction, that providing cattle to the peasantry was an offence to communist doctrine.

'Early in January,' I went on, 'you allowed two lambs to each peasant. But the fact is that most people refused them. They refused because they were not to be satisfied with so little. They want cows, and if you don't satisfy them, next year they'll want more than cows! You are backward in every sense. That is why your work is in vain, because what is given too late satisfies no one. The machine slips its gears, it simply idles—that's what is so appalling.'

I hammered away at the matter of supplying cows to the peasants with a stubbornness that might seem surprising, since I am considered a writer not versed in agricultural matters. But the question of cows is not just an agricultural problem. During the previous months I had spoken with journalists who'd been out in the provinces, as well as with economists and with eminent physicians. All of them gave the same painful report: the destitution of the peasants was unbearable, thousands of children had neither milk to drink nor meat to eat. Diseases previously unheard of had suddenly appeared as a consequence of malnourishment. That evil attacked the very foundation of the Albanian race. It was imperative that cows be distributed at once. Such a measure would bring renewed health not only to the country districts—representing two-thirds of the population—but to the entire nation. Neither sheep not goats could replace cows, and on no account should we be limited to goats, ewes and lambs.

While I was speaking I felt a strange, confused fury mounting inside me, fury at the very thought of those small livestock. The 'artist' in my brain had sounded the general alarm. That was the only way I could mount such an impassioned protest about a subject I had never thought about in this way. At that moment the caprine and ovine species seemed like wicked breeds to me—Stalinist breeds. So, only cows! If, in the Albanian literature of the past, pictures of cows were sacred, it was not by mere chance.

'Certainly you're familiar, Comrade Ramiz, with the famous passage by Migjeni in which the mountain folk, on a freezing night, lead a cow close to the fire on the hearth, and a baby dies of cold because of her. You know the manner in which they sing about the cow in the old ballad, *The Black Ox*?'

I had noticed that the age-old ballads are the best antidote to Stalinist dogma. In a sense they're always a protest. It's easy to believe that the people had conceived them with a clear purpose, which was to prepare themselves for difficult times.

The President seemed moved. Several people had put pressure on him to allow a redistribution of cattle, but I had the impression that I had given him the deciding impulse.

Without transition I took up the matter of foreign policy. Now more than ever, Albania needed to have direct relations with other countries. The problem of Kosovo alone was enough to sweep away all hesitation. The vicissitudes I had spoken of made such a measure obligatory. In the summer of 1989, after festivities marking the bicentennial of the French Revolution, I had lunch with President Mitterrand at the Elysée Palace, and stressed that the democratization of Albania, Kosovo, and Serbia was an integral part of a complex regional development. (I had had that interview with the French President without asking anyone's permission, which didn't sit well in Albania. That was obvious from the fact that the press never printed a word about it. Nevertheless, when I returned, no one criticized me directly, but showed disapproval by not asking me what I had discussed with Mr Mitterrand.)

Because of the troubles she faced, Albania needed to establish close diplomatic relations with the Soviet Union and with the United States. I mentioned both of the superpowers, but I particularly urged an opening to the United States—I was not unaware that the USSR already had its partisans among us: half the members of the Albanian

Central Committee could scarcely restrain their impatience for a *rapprochement* with the Soviets. On the other hand, no one yet dared to speak of the United States. For my part, I had long been regarded as a 'spokesman for the West', and far from trying to hide it, I made no effort to balance the scales. (Here is a detestable habit of East European bureaucracies: they pretend to regard both sides equally, but everyone knows that their attention is always directed to one side alone.)

I could not report to the President of Albania that in France, during the bicentennial ceremonies and profiting by the opportunity given me two days running as the personal guest of François Mitterrand, lunching and dining in the same hall with Heads of State, I had told President Bush that I was grateful for his country's support of the Albanians in Kosovo. And that I had also apologized for the fact that the Albanian press, feeling no sense of indebtedness at all, continued to attack the United States in a manner both graceless and mean.

Even so, I told my President these same things in a different way, reminding him that the United States was the only country to support Albania's cause at the beginning of the century; and now, at the century's end, we had an obligation either to show our gratitude or to go down in history as being fickle.

On this issue, too, I felt Ramiz Alia had taken the point. Then suddenly I saw among my notes the name Sofo Lazri. I had circled the name in red without further remark, for I needed no reminder. He was the chief, or perhaps the only, adviser to the President on foreign policy matters, known for his animosity to the intellectuals, and especially to the writers (even though he himself held the title 'professor'.) He was a slavophile, morbidly touchy, and generally considered a serious obstacle to Albania's contact with the outside world. I was certain that if I didn't steal a march on him, his jealousy would make him move heaven and earth to destroy the good effect of my conversation with the President.

It was nearly three o'clock, and I had neither the time nor the strength to find an elegant way to bring the conversation around to that man. So I opened the matter directly, without beating about the bush. 'I don't know what your advisers think about the various issues we've discussed, but I am certain that one, Sofo Lazri, given his hatred for writers, must be opposed to me on every point.'

He shook his head. 'He is my chief adviser, and he is very able.'

'He may be able, but you're probably not unaware that he cares little for the intelligentsia, and that the intelligentsia returns the favour.'

The President smiled. 'I must say that you, too, are not fair in all matters. I can tell you that, apropos of the United States, Lazri made the same argument, in precisely the terms you did—in fact, while you were speaking it occurred to me that you two had probably agreed beforehand to raise the issue.'

'I'm delighted,' I said. For an instant I felt remorse, but it didn't last. 'Naturally, I am delighted, and I'd be pleased if I were wrong on this count. However, I'm convinced that if he came to hear of our talk, he would strain every nerve to undo the measures I have suggested to you.'

The President smiled again. 'You're not being fair,' he said.

As a man who had succeeded in dealing with an unpleasant but necessary task, I hastened to move on to two other matters: Stalin and religion. I had raised these issues with him before, so they were relatively simple to deal with now. Here were two problems that could be resolved swiftly, problems that were injuring the reputation of Albania.

Throughout Albania and Kosovo, Stalin was hated. He had used derogatory language against the Albanian nation, language worthy of the bandit he was. That alone would have justified dropping him at once. His statues should be demolished, and his name buried once and for all.

As for religion, it was already avenging itself upon its persecutors. In the future, its vengeance might prove even more terrifying. That's why our mistake must be repaired at once. The Greeks were worried, with good reason, about their co-religionists living in Albania. Good ethnic relations between the two countries have been disrupted because of that bit of stupidity. We must reopen the churches, particularly for the Greek minority among us (who seem to be saying, 'We are a separate people; you—you can do what you want, but we want our churches.') Then we must make provision for Catholics in Shkodra, and for the other Christians. Our Muslims will want the mosques opened again, although I suspect they might be in less of a hurry than their fellow countrymen on this issue. I'm convinced that Albania will most likely embrace Christianity since it is linked to the country's culture, and to a nostalgic memory of the time before Turkish rule. In the coming years, Islam, which arrived late in Albania in the baggage of the Ottoman overlords, will weaken—first in Albania, and then in Kosovo. Christianity, or rather Christian culture, will hold its own throughout the country. In this way, one evil (the 1967 prohibition against religious practice) shall give birth to good. Albania will carry out a great rectification of history that will hasten its union with the mother continent—Europe.

He listened thoughtfully, not saying yes or no. It was nearly half past three. I asked him to excuse me for taking so much of his time, but he said it was of no importance. I tried to put before him as briefly as possible all that I still had to say. I returned to the issue of human rights, I spoke about political repression, about the psychoses that marked those inside the Sigurimi—particularly their mania for trickery and for spreading falsehoods to support the notion that they were the pillar without which the state would crumble. I reminded him that several of his ministers were abhorrent to the people, but said that I had not seen the least sign of an attempt to overthrow the state.

Shortly before four o'clock I left his office, conscious of the astonished stares of his secretary and bodyguards.

6

For some time I told no one about my interview with the President, let alone the matters we had discussed. I knew that if there was one thing that would put at risk all possibility of favourable change in Albania (Lord, how easy it was to ruin everything, to undo everything!) it would be premature rumours. A single word could bring down the whole fabric.

I looked intently for any sign of change as a result of that conversation. At first there was nothing. Then there were timid whispers about revising the penal code, about a new electoral law, about the appointment of another public prosecutor and a new Minister of Justice. Certainly other people must have worked to bring about these changes—putting in a word here, a word there; drafting letters, signed or perhaps anonymous; they would have put their careers in danger, perhaps more than their careers. But under conditions of general uncertainty, when everything was held in suspense, benumbed, stupefied, sunk in coma, I was sure that the impetus I had given to the Head of State would be decisive.

Rumours were followed by the freeing of several political prisoners. What other governments would do openly, in a display of magnanimity, the Albanian government did surreptitiously. The incarcerated people emerged from prison one by one, silently, as if tiptoeing out of the gateway so as not to awaken a wild beast.

Naturally, I took this to be a result of my meeting with Ramiz Alia. But one fine day, glancing through the newspaper, I said to myself, that is a decision that most certainly resulted from our discussion! The Minister of the Interior (why him, I wonder?) made public the number of political prisoners—some eighty people. In the course of our conversation, I raised that question with the President, telling him that there were murmurs of astounding figures, between five thousand and forty thousand.

Of course, very few people accepted the government's statistics, but it was of great importance that they be published. Announcing the number of prisoners, like announcing the number of people executed by firing squad (four people in the course of six years), was a clear indication that the regime wanted to reduce the number of prisoners detained and to abolish the death penalty. In a country where that position had previously been denounced as 'giving up the class struggle'—tantamount to treason—such a measure could not be taken lightly.

About Stalin, however, nothing was said. Nor was anything said about making religion legal. As for Albania's relations with the United States and the Soviet Union, one could pick up here and there only the faintest hint, cautious in the extreme.

I scarcely knew whether to be jubilant or humble when, one evening, this bit of news was announced on television: the peasants were to be given cows! My happiness was twofold. First, this was a just and a most important measure. Something for which so many people had gone to prison was now lawful, an accomplished fact. Second, it gave me hope about all the other issues. On 4 February, shaking my hand as we parted at the top of the stairway, the President had said to me, 'It will all be done.' Now I turned this phrase over in my mind like a man who examines a ring to judge its worth.

'You never told me that,' my wife said after hearing the resounding announcement on television. 'That is the first I've heard of it.'

'Really? I don't know why not. But it's certainly what he told me when he said goodbye.'

I tried to understand how those last words had escaped me, and wondered if I had simply let them slip out of memory. Little by little the explanation came to me. He had said those words quite without emphasis, with no attempt at rhetoric, without a smile—on the contrary, he had spoken as if careworn, in the tone of a man delivering news about which he is not very happy.

Nevertheless, even though he had spoken to me that way, quietly, without any socialist grandiloquence, little by little I had come to rely even more firmly on the promise of those words.

The next Sunday after the redistribution of cows and land, I went, as was my habit, to have coffee by the seaside in Durrës. The road from Tirana to Durrës was unusually busy.

The free trade in cows and other livestock had begun, the driver told me. At Shijak the great cattle market was open again. On either side of the road villagers were leading the cows and calves they had just bought. Others had loaded their animals onto carts. Now and then people rode by on motorcycles, the passenger in the rear seat holding a lamb in his arms.

I could barely contain my delight. This was no foolish innocence I felt! One has to have been a citizen in Eastern Europe, where change comes slowly, where one would wait months, even years, for improvement (that is, if improvement came at all), to understand what a miracle this was. On that day thousands of peasants had been given their cows. The next morning, they would have milk and butter on the table, and soon after cheese and meat. In the coming weeks, thousands of others would have the same pleasure, and it would spread everywhere in the same way. At least five hundred thousand children, whose bodies and spirits were languishing from lack of proper nourishment, would be given a fresh burst of life—and for the Albanian people, so few in number, that was an enormous triumph. It was as if France had been given milk and meat to feed eight million of its children!

No, my delight was anything but naive. With those cows and allotments of land, and with the sense of independence and dignity they restored to the peasantry, we were restoring their morale. It was not by accident that the dictatorship, like the old witches of past ages, had stopped the flow of milk—milk doled out miserably to its countless invisible enemies, because that was the food that nourished and sustained the nation. And now, the milk was back, and in a sense had warded off the spilling of blood.

In the afternoon, when we were returning from Durrës, the road was even more crowded. Near Shijak, our driver asked a man on foot, 'What were you doing in Shijak?' 'In Shijak?' the man said. 'Lord, what a market! I never saw anything like it, not even in a dream.'

Perhaps the original Albania had come to life again, not the old Albania but the eternal one, as described by D. Pasko. The Albania of great herds and markets where all the peoples of the Balkans came to buy, and where, far more than at international meetings and forums, the peoples of the world understood one another.

7

As I expected, a counter-offensive was not long in coming. The Sigurimi made every effort to slow the wheels of progress. Radio and television, both strongholds of the reactionaries, never let an opportunity slip to attack the United States. Nor did *The Voice of the People*.* In the same issue of the paper in which a paragraph reported the US Senate's condemnation of the oppression of Albanians in Kosovo, there were five hostile articles about the United States. I was having coffee at the Dajti** with M. Elezi, the newly named Press Director of the Central Committee, and I told him it was shameful, brutal, anti-Albanian, pro-Serb! He listened in earnest; I felt that he too was pained, but he had no answer for me. It meant that things were being decided higher up in the government. Most people felt that the source was the President's chief foreign policy adviser. Others denied it. (To tell the truth, in a system of that kind, there's no way to tell where the ill-will had been hatched.)

Everyone felt more or less in a state of paralysis. Delegations from the West went home irritated and empty-handed. Here and there, at the instigation of a handful of intellectuals whose services were for hire, a theory developed that Albania had no democratic traditions—hence the need to be vigilant, extraordinarily vigilant!

On the contrary, Albania has deep roots in the democratic tradition. She was the only Balkan country that, while in the bosom

---

* *Zeri e Popullit*, the daily newspaper of the Albanian Workers' Party.
** The largest hotel in Tirana.

of the Ottoman Empire, had been governed by her own ancient Code, in which certain basic principles, like equality before the law and respect for the individual (male), raised to the level of a cult, had taught people to live in a kind of democracy—one as primitive as it was tragic. For a short period beginning in 1924, the Albanian Republic was the most democratic state in the Balkans, and its President, the bishop and writer Fan Noli, was without doubt the most enlightened Head of State of his time.

In the matter of political traditions, what was there for Albania to be envious of in the traditions of Germany or Poland, let alone Hungary or the Soviet Union? The argument that Albania lacked democratic traditions was nothing more than a sordid pretext put forward by the party of oppression. It wasn't the first time that dogmatic intellectuals had thrown mud at their own people. All that mattered to them was helping the 'dictatorship of the proletariat'.

Meanwhile the pleasant news had turned most unpleasant. People had been caught writing leaflets, and they had been arrested. It was said that people were being murdered along the Albanian border. Every week the Sigurimi broadcast the rumour that conspiracies had been unearthed in far-off regions; they were investigated meticulously, but it turned out that there were no such conspiracies.

Reporters returning from the country spoke of their astonishment at seeing so many cows everywhere. How had people come by all those animals? The mystery was soon cleared up: thousands of cows and sheep had been hidden by the peasants in blockhouses and underground military works no longer in use. In expectation of the new cattle law, the animals had come forth from their secret hideaways. (At least those horrid bunkers served some good purpose.)

'It was wonderful to see,' a journalist told me. 'The cows staggered as they walked. I imagine their eyesight was ruined from living so long in the dark.'

I couldn't make out whether the story of the cows' ocular troubles was a journalistic exaggeration or not, but it did seem to make some sense.

The precarious situation, and the prevailing uncertainty, moved me to publish an interview in a journal for young people.

I felt it was important to give a new dimension to all the issues I had discussed with the President. Through that medium, I might give voice to the issues, circulate them, make them public, and thus accomplish more than by speaking behind closed doors. In short, it would be in a sense like bearing witness, and would provide an accounting for history. At the same time, it would carry a subtle threat: what was said between us was neither private nor something to be trampled under foot.

For a long time R. Lani, Editor-in-Chief of *The Voice of Youth*, had been asking me to give him an interview. One morning I picked up the phone and, to his surprise, told him I would grant him his interview in two days, and would answer some of his questions and add others of my own.

Forty-eight hours later I did in fact give him the interview, and gave him two short letters plus an 'odd' text. They left him dumbfounded.

Here are those letters. The first: *Dear R., Thank you for the understanding you showed in the interview.* The second: *Comrade R., I have read your comments, and I disagree absolutely. Publish the interview as it stands or return it to me immediately.*

The next day when we met for coffee, he was quite happy. The interview had pleased him; the two letters and the third text had amused him very much.

'As to your second letter, I mean to keep it as a souvenir, but I am not the type of man who would exploit it.'

Anyone who has dealt with the press knows that the first thing asked of an editor after publication of something that might be construed as unorthodox is whether or not the author had put pressure on him, especially if the author is well known. If he had, the Editor-in-Chief would be absolved of responsibility for the article, and the onus would lie with the author alone.

'You laugh now,' I said, 'but I warn you that the interview may get you into trouble. I'm quite serious. You may have to pay dearly for it, and not I. That's why . . . '

'No,' he said, 'I'm going to print your interview with an easy mind. I would tear up your second letter in your presence if I weren't determined to keep it as a souvenir. Now, that piece on the tribunal is a little wonder.'

He took it from his pocket to read again. It was a sketch I had written in a somewhat distracted state. Here it is:

Extract of a Session of the Mitrovista Tribunal, Tito District

Judge Zemfirovitch: I ask the accused, R. Lani, is it true that Ismail Kadare put pressure on you to publish this unwholesome memoir?

R. Lani: It is quite true. He did indeed put pressure on me, with fearful threats of a sort that mankind has not seen since 1732. Among other things, for example, he told me that he had taken steps to ensure that his vengeance would pursue me even after his death. He even prophesied that after my own death, someone would come to pillage my tomb every three years.

Judge Zemfirovitch: I ask the accused, Ismail Kadare, is this true?

I. Kadare: It is not only false, but the contrary is true. R. Lani made me promise under oath that I would give him an interview. Not only did he plead for it, but when he saw that I was hesitant, he declared that if I did not grant him an interview immediately, he would throw himself from the tenth floor of his apartment building, just facing the far side of the neighbouring hospital, so that the emergency squad would come too late.

We laughed about that. The little playlet, though somewhat grotesque, had its basis in truth. At Mitrovista, in the Tito district of Yugoslavia, an endless lawsuit was still being tried. The title of the piece, as well as the judge's Serbian surname, made no sense from one point of view. But from another, looking at it as a writer's brainchild, it was full of truths, even though those truths were not always explicit.

The interview made the stir that I had expected, and more. That confirmed my feeling that it had come at the right time. The piece represented only some of the issues I had raised with the President; as it happened, they were the least unsettling ones, and rather more prudent in their presentation. But it was enough to draw wide attention—especially to the invisible part of the iceberg, drowned and putrid in the icy depths and the darkness.

The interview started a four-alarm fire. Tens of thousands of copies of the journal were sold instantly; people photocopied them, Gypsies sold them on the black market. One would think that everyone had come back to life. Little by little voices were raised in protest. Timidly at first (people were waiting for a signal from the authorities), then more openly. The protest, understandably, came first from some high-ranking members of the Sigurimi—but, another surprise, others of that group abstained. There were a number of officials, many district administrators, and, to sum up, all sorts of idiots who on every pretext and every issue, banded together against me. The absence of any sign from the highest quarters was disconcerting, for those people had been used to getting signs. For that reason their accusations lacked the virulence of earlier times. ('Well, *he* is no longer with us. He would have known just what to do with Ismail Kadare'—that's what was being whispered in the corridors of the Central Committee. *He* was Enver Hoxha, evoked in the most contradictory fashion, depending on the shape that each debate took—sometimes as my protector, sometimes as my persecutor, and sometimes as my projected assassin.)

Two accusations were levelled at me. One seemed harmless ('He's doing that because he wants the Nobel Prize') compared with the other, which was dangerous in the extreme: 'He wants to be President, like Vaclav Havel.' The latter became more and more embarrassing, hobbling me, because any action, any word, unfailingly provoked some malicious comment. (Well, he said that in imitation of Havel. Sure, he did that in order to create an opposition party, like Havel.)

Havel became my torment, and it offered a perfect springboard for them. The could trip me up whenever they chose, and do what I might I would take a fall each time.

Unfortunately, foreign journalists fanned the flames with their speculations. I thought with a kind of terror that the Head of State might be reading the *Special Bulletin*, which published foreign articles in translation. My terror grew when I learned that his advisers were also saying things like, 'Another piece of work à la Havel. Let's see how this one turns out . . .'

One can imagine the rich vein that the Sigurimi could exploit at my expense. It would not be difficult for them to embark on investigations that would allow them to establish that 'hostile elements and a number of naive people', encouraged by the position I had taken, wanted to make me President—which comes to saying that I was potential enemy number one of the present government.

In its campaign against me the Sigurimi found a new ally, a certain Arshi Pipa, an Albanian writer who had fled to the United States in 1960. He was interviewed on the Albanian broadcast of *The Voice of America*, in which he expressed his disagreement with my position. His thesis was that writers like Ismail Kadare, who had appeared during the communist regime in Albania, had no right to speak of democracy.

That was not the first time that he had censured me, and other intellectuals as well. A little earlier, he had attacked Tozaj's novel *The Knives*, as well as my review of it. Pipa's criticism took this form: 'The author, N. Tozaj, and his protector, Ismail Kadare, are not telling the truth when they denounce the Albanian Sigurimi. There is no point in blaming the Sigurimi. The Party is to blame. Since they do not have the courage to attack the Party openly, they have no right to speak at all.' Now, Arshi Pipa knew perfectly well that it was not possible to attack the Party in the summer of 1989, not only in Albania but in most of the countries of Eastern Europe. In writing and publishing his novel, Tozaj had risked his life, and Arshi Pipa, with a mean and mendacious argument, had the audacity to declare that the novel had been written by order of the Sigurimi itself!

Using the same logic, one could find many reasons for turning the accusation of collaborating with the Sigurimi against Arshi Pipa himself. In putting forward the notion that the Albanian intellectuals who grew up under the communist regime had no right to take part in the process of democratizing the country, he was attempting to paralyse those intellectuals—a feat that even the Sigurimi and the Party dogmatists never dreamed would be accomplished.

In an interview I gave on *The Voice of America*, I felt obliged to mention a bitter memory I owe to Arshi Pipa. That was the 'study' he wrote about me in the early 1980s, when I was at the edge of the precipice. In that interview I spoke of the study as 'a denunciation, a calumny, an act of espionage for the benefit of the secret police.' And that was the absolute truth, as I explained in *Invitation to the Writer's Studio*.[4]

Of course, my answer to Arshi Pipa did not please the Albanian officials, including the President, who pointed it out expressly in his letter to me of 21 May.[*]

The matter of deciding who should take up the process of democratization if we must exclude the intellectuals—the brains of the nation—has posed difficulties for Arshi Pipa and other charlatans of that stripe. By his actions, this failed writer has simply shown once more that the bitter envy of mediocre artists represents, in this sublunary world, the bad seed from which neither the passing of millennia, nor the changes of manners, ideologies, and epochs, nor even the widespread humanization of civilized society, can free us.

---

[*] See pages 102–107.

8

April, the month of love in the old Albanian tradition (*March is gone with its rough airs/April smiles on love affairs . . .*), could hardly have been described in that manner in 1990. Taking advantage of the President's hesitation and the void it created, the Minister of the Interior increased the pressure.

In actual fact, irresolute decisions and contradictory measures had never been so much in evidence. Every initiative was abandoned after three or four days. Every action was followed by a 'but . . .' People felt that ballast should be jettisoned so as not to let the balloon fall too swiftly. But there was also another philosophy current: if you do nothing at all, you'll fall just the same. The image of Ceauçescu, with that tragic necktie at his throat, was in everyone's mind.

'They're going to take away the bust of Stalin from the Academy,' the secretary of the institution told me one day. 'But they're not going to replace it with Gjon Buzuk,* as you suggested in your interview.'

That example is significant, and it really was 'the time of *but . . .,*' as someone has christened it. People tried to satisfy the 'two camps', the 'two blocs'. The Bible passage, 'Rejoice not, thou who art joyful; weep not, thou who art sorrowful,' seemed to have been written expressly for that time. They arrested people and beat them in the police stations, *but* they released them after two or three days. (Before, perhaps, they were not so quick to beat the people they had

---

* The monk who, in 1555, wrote the first known book in the Albanian language.

arrested, *but* they didn't release them either. Now, however, they beat them, *but* they released them; or again, they released them, *but* they beat them.)

With this game of miserly compensations, the government could claim that it had finally discovered the golden mean.

Taking advantage of all this fog, the Minister of the Interior demanded, 'because of "the critical situation,"' that an unprecedented measure be adopted: the right to keep a prisoner under close surveillance—not for three days, as the law prescribed, but for fourteen days. That was a cynical offensive on the part of obscurantist forces, calculated, it would seem, in keeping with the theory of *buts*, so as to have at least half of the extended term adopted.

The People's Assembly was due to be in session ten days later. The deputy Ylli Popa, a well-known physician and scientist, managed to block the bill, at least in the Committee on Health.[5] Two other committees rejected it as well. It was the first time that any bill had been rejected by the People's Assembly. But the minister Simon Stefani argued in its favour in the Politburo, of which he was a member—and the Politburo swept away the objections of the deputies.

The Ministry of the Interior, and especially its most sinister arm, the Sigurimi, were in seventh heaven. One day, before the Assembly had gone into session, the head of the Sigurimi, Zylyftar Ramizi, the right-hand man of Simon Stefani and one of the most hated people in the country, stopped his car on the Grand Boulevard to tell one of my friends, 'Two or three days from now I'll have that law allowing fourteen days' detention. He'll see, your writer friend, and others like that doctor, Ylli Popa.'

Meanwhile, not having heard of the episode, I had written a long letter to the President.[*]

I decided to write to him when I felt convinced that the danger of turning back the clock was growing day by day. The People's

---

[*] See pages 108–112.

Assembly was scheduled to meet on Monday. On the preceding Saturday my letter was ready, but the President had not yet returned from his trip to the southern part of the country. I heard that he was to be back in the evening.

Late in the afternoon, I telephoned his secretary. They had just returned, and I told him what was troubling me. I wanted the President, at any cost, to read my letter before the Assembly went into session. The secretary promised without hesitation, and we agreed that I would give him the letter the following day—Sunday.

We met at ten o'clock in the morning at the Hotel Dajti. After a cup of coffee we parted. It was 10:45. 'I'm going to take it to him directly, at his home,' the secretary said as he took the letter. 'He should have it by eleven.'

On Monday morning, an hour before the opening of the Assembly session, the government held an emergency meeting. I was glad to think that the meeting had something to do with my letter, but I did not feel that I should celebrate too soon.

We were all waiting expectantly. And what a surprise—really a surprise, a rare moment—we had lost nothing by waiting for it: authorization to travel abroad freely; the plan to renew relations with the United States and the Soviet Union; rejection of the fourteen-day surveillance bill; a slight hope for freedom of worship; private property; credit; and the amendment of various articles of the constitution. Without question, something had been accomplished!

The next day (the Assembly meanwhile continued in session), my friend N. Tozaj, to whom I had shown my letter, phoned me around noon.

'Congratulations! One of your *seven* has fallen. Good luck! I bet they'll all fall now.'

The Assembly declared a recess, and there was a sudden report that the President of the Supreme Court—one of the most sinister figures of the time—had resigned. He was among the seven officials whom I had excoriated by name in my letter to the President (the others were Rita Marko, the Vice-President of the Republic; Zylyftar

Ramizi, Chief of National Security; the Attorney-General; the Director-General of the Police; and two sadists of the Sigurimi in Tirana.)

That gave me no small pleasure. Even though people had long been raising other important issues, discussing, trying to apply pressure—the more so because we were on the eve of Pérez de Cuellar's visit—the quashing of the fourteen-day bill and the forced resignation of the President of the Supreme Court had something to do with my letter. It meant that the letter had been welcome, and it gave me hope that at last we might retire all those fossilized officials who were strangling the country.

Three days later, the two Sigurimi sadists from Tirana were dismissed. The fact was not hidden from them that their dismissal was somehow tied to a letter to the President sent by Ismail Kadare.

That procedure had never been adopted before. Enraged by the treatment of their colleagues, other members of the Sigurimi cursed me openly: 'We'll show him what we're made of.' The two men who had been sacked strutted through the streets and drank coffee at the Hotel Dajti with their comrades in arms, sometimes with the head of the Sigurimi himself, the all-powerful Ramizi.

For myself, I missed no opportunity to inveigh against them. Not only was the joy of the first victory beginning to fade but I was very much embittered; it seemed intolerable that having written the letter, Ramizi was still in office. I felt it so deeply that one day, at the Hotel Dajti—where everyone knew that conversations were recorded as a matter of course—I told my friends, 'If Mr Ramizi isn't fired, I'll have to see about leaving Albania!'

At this time, Pérez de Cuellar, whose coming to Albania was of great moment to all sorts of people for all sorts of reasons, arrived in Tirana. Some persons were expecting great things as a result of his visit. Others could scarcely hold back their tears: 'They'll pull the wool over his eyes, they'll take him into camp with fine promises, and everything will remain the same in the government.' Indeed, it was reasonable to surmise that the new measures were part of the show for his benefit, and that once he had departed there would be a renewed repression, even worse than before.

I did not hold with either group. The first annoyed me with their bleating optimism that betrayed a good dose of repressed conformism. But the others were no less irritating; their every remark began, 'I told you so. Nothing will change.' And it was a close call if they were not impatient to see their prophecies come true. They were prepared to see things go from bad to worse just so they might crow over the ruins and misery—'I told you so.'

I had become acquainted with Pérez de Cuellar in Paris, at a meeting of the Academy of Moral and Political Science, in which both of us took part. I met him again at a reception at the Palais des Brigades. Though we spoke only briefly, de Cuellar said to me in the presence of the Prime Minister and the Albanian Minister of Foreign Affairs, that of all my books *The Niche of Shame* was the one he liked best, and that he was reading *The Concert*—a detail that astonished the head of the diplomatic service.

'I'm surprised that you've read those books,' he said, aghast. 'When you consider that the United Nations has some hundred and fifty member states . . .'

'My dear Minister, I have no obligation to read the novels of the one hundred and fifty member countries,' de Cuellar replied. 'I read for pleasure.'

Most of the time during that reception in his honour, Pérez de Cuellar was talking in a corner with Ramiz Alia. No doubt other members of the Albanian contingent would have liked to make his acquaintance and profit a bit from his company, but they were happy to abstain and instead enjoy watching him keep up that long conversation with our President. Let them talk face to face about the most important issues, as candidly as possible!

9

The aircraft bearing the United Nations banner had scarcely taken off when here below, on earth, where things are always more burdensome, the question arose: Now what will happen?

For a time, nothing, only a blank period of waiting. Then the first sign—a bad one.

In Korça, during a meeting of staff officials, Rita Marko, a member of the Politburo and number two in the government hierarchy, was the first to explode about the guests who had just departed.

'Well, now, Pérez de Cuellar, you think that you can give us lessons: we have the teachings of Enver Hoxha, and we don't need any others. People like de Cuellar come and go.'

That was the language of the hoodlum—especially here, in a country where, generation after generation, an affront to a guest was punished by death.

Besides being one of the most incompetent and ignorant officials in the Politburo (several had not reached high-school) Rita Marko was a *shule*, a person not of Albanian stock, and this was no matter of mere chance. The Albanians, no angels when it comes to racism, scornfully call the Macedonians who live in Albania (some four to five thousand people) '*shule*'. Although the Albanians have no right whatsoever to despise their fellow man—a quite unacceptable trait—one must admit that there is something odd here. It is strange indeed that in the country of the 'Sons of the Eagle', who during certain historical periods had governed the colossal Ottoman Empire, the despised *shule* had always played a not unimportant role among the governing elite. Generally speaking, in the modern Politburo, a quarter or even a third of the members have been *shule* or Wallachians.

The notorious Koçi Xoxe comes to mind—Enver Hoxha's second-in-command. He too was a *shule*. It's been said that while he was in prison, before being condemned to death, he declared, 'You accuse me of not loving Albania, but I don't have to love her, I'm a Bulgarian!' Whatever his origins, it's obvious that things had not come about by coincidence. Whether chosen by the Comintern or by Enver Hoxha, the *shule* and the Wallachians suited the communist regime perfectly because since they had no ties to the Albanian nation, they felt no compassion for her. You could tell them, 'Strike without mercy!' And their arm never trembled, they struck down everything—the nation's history, her people, her very foundations. With great fervour they crippled the proud Albanian race. In their zeal and their thirst for revenge, their sense of inferiority played an important part.

Here is a very real problem, to which the Albanian people—who are very particular in matters of race and national ties when marriages are in question, but not about politics—have given very little conscious attention. That oversight is one of several that have cost them dear.

Another hateful person, Muho Asllani, formerly a wheelwright in a cooperative, at present a member of the Politburo, also inveighed against Pérez de Cuellar in language that any drunken wheelwright would have envied.

Was it just another coincidence that the Sigurimi and the most reactionary people in the Politburo, people like Lenka Çuko, Prokop Murra, Simon Stefani and Vangjel Çerrava, that collection of illiterates, imbeciles and Ostrogoths, all joined in the hostile chorus against our distinguished guests? (Later, at a meeting between a group of intellectuals and the President, following the tragic events of July, I reminded Ramiz Alia that the new disappointment felt by the people which had led to the riot, had begun on the very day that high-ranking officials had spilled their bile upon Pérez de Cuellar.

The President claimed that this was the first he had heard of it. Most of those present did not believe him.)

That time of expectation, one of the most detestable in dictatorial regimes, lasted quite a while. It was hard to see how the void could be filled. Would there be another turn of the screw, or would there be a certain relaxation? The signs could be taken to favour one or the other hypothesis. At the Academy of Science they removed the bust of Stalin. At night, taking precautions. So as not to offend that murderer, they did not replace it with the bust of the monk Gjon Buzuk, as I had proposed, and perhaps so as not to offend me (me!) they did not replace it with the bust of Fan Noli, which the Academy had suggested. At Shkodra they also took away the bust of Stalin—in daylight, with a crane, in full view of the crowd. An amusing anecdote—a passer-by told the gardener responsible for the flowers growing at the now unoccupied base, 'Don't water them. *He* might spring up again'—put the final touch to a painful story that had swallowed up the lives of many people.

But the dismantling of the statues, like everything else, had come too late, so late that no one was satisfied. Holding back was once more in fashion. It was the conduct of a miser, dragging things out was a way to gain time. One would have thought that the clocks of the Albanian government had all stopped.

The sense that things were frozen was mitigated by the regime's latest preoccupation—worrying about balance. To counter-balance the removal of the busts so that the reactionaries would not despair, they sent out delegations to deal with economic questions, and sent them empty-handed. (It might have happened in just the other way; after sending out the delegations empty-handed to please the reactionaries, they might then have disgusted them by taking away more busts!) Every project came to nothing: oil prospecting at sea with the Germans or the Norwegians, construction of a highway, of an international airport, the opening of stores stocked with foreign products, or of a chain of three hundred fast-food restaurants, etc.

Contradictory news reports and speeches completed the scene. Don't you think that surveillance has been relaxed somewhat, or contrarily that the Sigurimi has redoubled its vigilance? Ramiz Alia has brought the reactionaries to their knees. Foto Çami[6] is responsible for the deterioration of relations with the Federal Republic of Germany during his visit there. Or, on the contrary, the relations that Foto Çami had more or less re-established with the GDR have been purposefully compromised by the President's adviser, Sofo Lazri, of sorry reputation, who went behind their backs to do it. It's Nexhmije Hoxha[*] who's pulling all the strings. That's just not so, the reins have slipped out of her hands. As for *him*, he's lost his marbles. But how about the poisoning of his dog? Isn't that a real threat, poisoning a dog? Good Lord! What poisoning? What dog? Some day this will drive us all round the bend.

The incident that brought me into conflict with Nexhmije Hoxha is typical of the atmosphere in those days.

The meeting of the Albanian Democratic Front, of which she was President and I was Vice-President, was supposed to approve a report she had drawn up for the Presidium's yearly meeting. After two speakers had said flattering things, I took the floor and said that I did not agree with the report, since it was not conceived in the spirit of the last plenum of the Central Committee on the democratization of the country.

I was giving my reasons for disagreeing when, in a voice trembling with emotion, she interrupted me.

'I will state my views later on, but I want to say now that I deplore the fact that you, Comrade Kadare, are joining the chorus of our domestic enemies and our foreign enemies, and that you have chosen me recently as a target, as if I were in some sense an obstacle to democratization.'

'I never said anything of the kind,' I replied.

'That's exactly what you said.'

'I said nothing of the sort. Read the transcript of my remarks.'

The twenty-five members of the Front, one of the country's most

---

[*] Enver Hoxha's widow.

conservative bodies, of which I was unfortunate enough to be Vice-President, abashedly followed the altercation that would have been inconceivable in the past. For them, nothing could have been more intolerable, more charged with foreboding, than that exchange of apocalyptic rejoinders. Particularly since there were just the two of us, she and I, at the head of the table, seated side by side—in a position most unsuited for confrontation.

'I beg your pardon,' she said. 'Excuse me for interrupting you. Do go on.'

I spoke for some twenty minutes, mostly about human rights. I declared without equivocation that in Albania, contrary to what the press said, contrary to what was written in the report, human rights were being trampled upon. I spoke of the complaints I had received as Vice-President of the Front, complaints of arrests, of beatings of those arrested, of assassinations at our borders, and of the people who had come to show me their backs, black and blue from the blows of police clubs.

'Haven't you received complaints like this?' I said, addressing the President of the Front for the city of Tirana.

He mumbled 'No,' through clenched teeth.

'That's too bad,' I said. 'It means that no one has confidence in you.'

I ended by telling all the things that I had discussed with the President. I also wanted to hear the opinions of the Presidium on these matters.

At the end of my speech I expected that the assembled presidents would fall upon me like madmen. That was what I had expected, and for that reason I had managed to keep cool. I had meant to tender my resignation after the battle with the presidents, in order to put an end to a misunderstanding that had troubled me for much too long.

'The floor is yours, comrades,' said Nexhmije Hoxha.

But to my astonishment (and even more I imagine to hers) the silence lasted an unusually long time. At last it was broken, but not in the way I had anticipated. One after another, the members who spoke approved the President's report, '*but*,' they said, on the other hand, 'the remarks of Comrade Kadare, a specialist in this matter, must also be taken into account.' Alas, our committee was acting in the spirit of the times! Compromise, duality!

Several members, among them the new Press Director of the Central Committee, explicitly said that they shared my views. (It now appears that the new Press Director, M. Elezi, paid for this act of courage; though he was not censured, he was dismissed from his post some weeks later.) Nexhmije Hoxha showed how clever she was. When she took the floor again, to everyone's astonishment (this meeting was rich in surprises), she declared that she understood now that her report was a bad one. She thanked the assembled presidents, and thanked me personally for my observations, noting, however, her disappointment at the tone I had taken in responding to her.

And that was how the meeting ended, the second and last such meeting of the Presidium of the Albanian Democratic Front in which I had taken part, and it was a gathering much discussed in the foreign press.

A few days later, Nexhmije Hoxha sent me a copy of her revised report, and a letter in which she begged my pardon for the misunderstanding. When I returned the report, I apologized for my breach of good manners.

The incident was much discussed in Tirana, but, submitting once more to the theory of balances, I had the uncomfortable feeling that I would pay dearly for it. From that day on, I was on the wrong side of the scale.

The gossip in the cafés could only fan the fire. People said that the Sigurimi had a good deal to do with that. Something will happen soon. Ramiz Alia is isolated again. Ramiz Alia is nothing of the kind—Nexhmije Hoxha is under arrest.

Part of that double consciousness was expressed in the slogans that were written on the walls at night. Among them, next to the words, 'Long live Ramiz Alia!', which was adopted by both the opponents of the government as well as its defenders, quite different sentiments began to appear: 'Down with Ramiz Alia!' Moreover, as someone pointed out to me, sometimes these had been written in the same hand; which, having set down the word 'Long . . .', had crossed it out and substituted 'Down with . . .!'

10

My misgivings proved to be justified. On the afternoon of 21 May, when the telephone rang and an unknown voice said, 'President's office. There's some material for you,' it was as if I had known it all along.

A letter came, one I was not expecting. I would have liked it to come months later, years later, never. That letter would change my life.

When my wife found me counting the number of times the word 'Party' appeared in the letter, she was afraid. As she told me later, 'I had never seen you so calm, so moved, so desperate, so gay, so sullen. It was as if you were—how can I put it? As if you were not quite human.'

Time seemed to have frozen. I sipped my coffee slowly, then said, 'Guess how many times the word "Party" appears in the letter.'

'How many?'

'Twenty-three times.'

In the street, half an hour later, we spoke about leaving, very much subdued, as if we were in the presence of death.

I was thinking that I had done everything in my power to bring about a relaxation of the government. I had told myself that the day the totalitarian state agreed to live with a genuine literature would be the first real sign of reform, of the regime's attempt to humanize itself. Through my work, I've held this dream up to the Albanian people and to thousands of readers around the world. Now I understood that, although there is something authentic in the dream, the illusion was no more than an illusion. To make it a reality there had to be some new impulse, a new dimension. That impulse would be my *absence*.

Who is not aware of the power of absence, of shadows, of phantoms? It's not by chance that our earliest ballads (*Songs of Absence and Return*) were dedicated to that theme. If my presence in Albania only hindered that which I sought to accomplish through my books, I must leave. A million copies of my books, scattered among a population of three and a half million, could serve their function just as easily without me. Indeed, if I were no longer inside the country, I could exercise more influence upon it. What I could not accomplish here, fully immersed in the situation, I could accomplish elsewhere, from a distance.[7]

In trying to create something better, I had trusted in the breaking up and wasting away of a world that had become more and more unbearable: a world of slogans, parades, festivals, misery, of articles crammed with directives, of Party instructors and the brutality of Party militants, of lying, hypocrisy, and boredom. But this world had proved to be more solidly built than I had realized. Something more was required to move things forward—absence, I thought, and its dimension of blindness would heighten the impact of my books. Like blindness, absence might confer a fresh sensibility and radiance, a radiance that the patina of time had dimmed. Thus renewed, my books and the books of my colleagues, and the whole of the new culture developing in Albania, might cast a splinter of doubt into that absurd universe, with its façade of liveliness and its pretence of assurance. And perhaps that would bring about a reopening of the case, opening it to shame, to remorse, to repentance.

That would be the beginning of real emancipation. And it would be the only way for change to come without bloodshed. Even if I was only dreaming, and if, despite everything, our illusions faded, I still believed in that outcome—it was proof that I still had hope, hope that the evil had not rooted itself too deeply in the country. For at every level of society, from ordinary citizens to the Head of State, one could find goodness, and could gather it together.

That's what I was thinking about on the morning of 21 May.

Other issues, such as the attempt by security forces to discredit me, the slander, the twisted reports of declarations I had never made—I regarded as ridiculous. As ridiculous as the threats of the Sigurimi, to which I was by this time fairly accustomed. No, those things were not enough to lead a man to take the step I had chosen. Something else led me in that direction, something deeper, something more timeless.

Discarding my last doubts, I had finally asked, in my innermost heart: Had I not turned again and again in my books to the theme of the man half alive, half dead? Had I not identified myself with that man? It seemed to me that he had served as the sign of a fate clearly marked. And I had to yield.

To flee . . .

It's a temptation that presents itself, one way or another—and even if only for a moment—to most Albanians. It had happened to me twice. The first time was in the summer of 1962, in Prague, when I was returning from Finland. The Albanian dictatorship was intolerable, but my motives were simple. Monthly military training, endless meetings, slogans like 'In everything, everywhere, we must conserve,' and 'We'll eat grass if necessary to defend Marxism-Leninism,' etc—I found it all mortifying and exasperating. On top of everything, the obligatory haircut was being talked about more and more frequently, and for me, this was a sign of the end. Poisoning people's lives is a routine function of dictatorship, and the poison let out through this obligatory haircut would not be unleashed little by little. On several occasions hair became the battlefield on which thousands of young Albanians confronted the state. The dictatorship meant to shorten their hair, and they were determined to let it grow. The regime was mining a vein of psychosis that probably came from a prison mentality, with its doctrine that hair was a form of evil. To make everyone look alike, to break their spirit, they had to begin with a uniform haircut and clothing—a technique perfected by the Chinese. Any refusal was considered to be the first step towards resistance, and was ruthlessly suppressed. (The Albanian government eventually decided to internationalize this annoying hairstyle and set up a barber at the Rinas airport!)

A Chronicle

You will understand my naivety when I tell you that I considered fleeing . . . to the Soviet Union! Despite my hesitation—I was, after all, bound to my family and to a student I'd met (my future wife)—what attracted me to Moscow, over and above escaping from hair troubles, were a couple of Russian girls . . .

And so, with my impermissibly long hair, threatening and bristling like a brush, I took French leave of the group I'd been travelling with. But my tiny hotel room was enough to make me change my plans. After fooling around for two or three hours in the streets of Prague, I found a room not far from Wenceslas Square. It was evening. After a tiring day I thought I would just lie down a bit. But once I was horizontal, I could see that the room was painfully ugly. I had the feeling that, little by little, it was getting smaller, more oppressive, like a grave. I got up not quite knowing what to do, and I left. I paced the streets like a sleepwalker. I reached Wenceslas Square and caught a tram which took me to, well, another hotel, where I found my original room. Thinking about nothing and not answering my roommate—the painter V. Kilica, who asked me how the devil I'd managed to disappear all day—I slept like a log. (The next morning he said to me, 'I saw you run off, but don't worry, nobody noticed and I told everyone that you were in a shop somewhere.' A wonderful man. He's never mentioned that episode again!)

With the passing of time, when I think hard about what might have become of me had I left that day, I'm haunted by the realization that none of my novels would have been written (at that time I had published only two or three collections of poems). I shudder to think that so much is contingent upon so little in this world, that the size of a hotel room built a hundred years ago could influence the literature of another country a century later.

You may believe me when I say that I've often blessed the unknown Czech architect whose style and lack of imagination, or perhaps his mediocre talent, gave birth to that ghastly hotel.

I was tempted to flee once again in November 1983, but that time for very serious reasons. Following a quarrel with the regime that went on throughout 1982, I began receiving daily death threats, allegedly from local hoodlums. I have described this dark period in a chapter of my book, *Invitation to the Writer's Studio*, the only thing that I dared publish on the subject.[8] During dinner at the Coupole in Paris on a cold November night, I told Michel Piccoli and his wife about my troubles, the first persons in whom I had confided such things. We discussed the problem from every angle, and in the end we decided that I ought to return to Albania.

Later, I was grateful to my old friends; if it hadn't been for their advice I would not have written *The Black Year*, *Moonlight*, *The Pyramid of Cheops*, *Aeschylus*, *Invitation to the Writer's Studio*, or the final versions of *The Concert* and *The Monster*.[9]

On my third and final flight, on 27 September 1990, when I set foot again on French soil, one of the first questions I asked myself was, 'How many books will be lost, before ever being written?'

Well, that is something that no one can know. Something that perhaps no one should know, and for that reason, no one need repine.

What came over you? What impulse made you write such foolishness?

Though I had buried the President's letter somewhere in my files, intending never to read it again, the words come back to me time and time again. I simply cannot recognize him in that letter. Had he really written it, or was it one of his colleagues? I often thought of Sofo Lazri (his use of the expression 'three thousand words' to demonstrate familiarity with the formulae of American journalism made me suspicious). The flood of words like 'Party' and 'Enver Hoxha', words the President hadn't used, even in public speeches, for a long time, words from the old tin ear of the bureaucracy that he himself had ridiculed, words that suggested a return to a time now over and done with, depressed and dismayed me. I kept telling myself that my astonishment might not be justified, it might be just the remnants of naive hopes and unpardonable illusions. Perhaps he had always been hard, dictatorial, with no sense of the whole. Had I overestimated his strength of character? Was I, like a drowning man, grasping at straws to preserve my feelings about him?

I quickly cast aside my doubts. I might be wrong, but how could hundreds of thousands of people have been led astray, people who two months earlier would have gone through fire and water for him? People who wrote on the walls at night, 'Down with dictatorship! Long live Ramiz Alia!' And how could so many political prisoners delude themselves and write to me proclaiming, 'At this time, he is our only hope'?

In a kind of waking dream the question pursued me relentlessly: What came over you? You were more fortunate than Gorbachev—he was more highly regarded outside his country than within it, but you, you could have been esteemed as much at home as abroad.

Sometimes the question went deeper, plunging into a dark abyss: What stopped you, what was it that held you back?

The poisoning of his dog, that had been hinted at within government circles, came to mind. It did indeed look like a first warning, and was tied to other rumours of blackmail—or to be more precise, to a written deposition somewhere, testimony against him that amounted to blackmail. And that was not far removed from the false rumours being peddled everywhere, both within the country and outside it, that predicted his assassination.

Could all that have started the poisoning of a dog?

The next morning, a time when ordinary things lose all their drama, that letter made a sinister impression upon me. Suddenly, I was aware of another dimension to what was wrong. The letter lacked any sense of a future, or of history. The man who had written it had made it clear that he was not concerned with such things. I found that not only troubling, but dangerous.

Yes, that was the message expressed in the letter, a thought that was particularly sinister, *dangerous*.

I was in a difficult situation—between Scylla and Charybdis. On the one hand, people were demanding more and more of me each day. On the other, the government had kept me under constant surveillance.

The shadow of Vaclav Havel never left me. It pushed in two directions—it inspired the crowd who swarmed in around me, and it constantly goaded the President. (For communists, there is a point at which they lose their reason and their vision. That point is power.)

He must act like Havel. He can't possibly be like Havel. He is no Havel.

But even if I had wanted to, I was in no position to share Havel's destiny. In my preface to Migjeni I had explained that there is a kind of dictatorship under which a well-known writer cannot find his way to prison; that is because he has lost his last chance. If the prison gates are closed to him, all that remain are the gates of hell.

My friends and people who wished me well often said, 'Watch out, the trap is closing in on you. Don't you see it?' At the same time the other chorus intoned the old refrain: 'Havel . . . Not Havel . . .' Foreign journalists often joined in, among them bar-room regulars who waited for something dramatic without realizing that the actors they were watching might die on stage, as in Alberto Moravia's play in which a Jewish amateur Thespian troupe performs *Oedipus Rex* in a concentration camp; the actors have their eyes put out and really die as the audience watches.

They wanted to know if I would ever become another Pasternak, a Havel, a Sakharov, an X or a Y, but no one ever thought to turn the question around: Could those men ever get to be like me?

They compared me with dissidents who had written during the post-dictatorial period, that is, at a time when the regime was relaxing; they forgot that I had written my books under the dictatorship, in the heart of the dictatorship, in the very depths of its night. I was one of the few writers of this half-century to have not simply provided genuine intellectual nourishment to my countrymen under these conditions, but to have provided that nourishment in quantity, ensuring that it became a prevalent feature of Albanian life. What I had accomplished was paradoxical in the extreme: a country under the 'dictatorship of the proletariat' had at its disposal a literary culture that was universal in scope, and comparable to that enjoyed by the most advanced nations of the world—advanced, that is, in liberty and civic freedom. Welcome to some people, disturbing to others, that paradox brought with it a train of misunderstandings and questions: What is this enigma? How did the writer manage it? And who deserves the credit? Or, by some chance, would that man have us believe that dictatorship is not so bad after all?

Most certainly, the credit does not go to the regime. But false modesty aside, my firm conviction is that the credit is not mine alone. It belongs chiefly to the Albanian people, to the entire Albanian nation wherever it is to be found, a nation which in a thousand ways—ways I find difficult to classify and count—knew how to safeguard those works of art.

One must love a people to understand it. Many people don't trouble themselves with such trifles. It is a matter of indifference to them whether or not a nation has access to things of the mind. Indeed, from a certain point of view (which has been discussed in the press) literature born under dictatorship runs counter to the scheme already worked out in their brain, so they do not mind seeing it suppressed.

The feeling of prostration that had been with me for so long, and that had probably moved me to write my book *Aeschylus*, assailed me now on every side.

What should I do? ('You must stay in Albania, even if they crucify you like Christ,' wrote Adam Demaçi, the writer and martyr of Kosovo, in an open letter after I'd left the country. How was I to explain to my colleague that the crucifixion—to which I had alluded several times in my last book, *Invitation to the Writer's Studio*—itself requires some degree of democracy: a forum, a press which is more or less free, a public trial? Where could one find that luxury in a totalitarian state? Is it simply by chance that no one was crucified in the forty years of Stalin's reign? And what shall we say of Albania? You cannot be crucified under a dictatorship. You can be *killed* like Jesus, but never crucified like him.)

But a cowardly assassination is only a partial evil. As soon as they had announced the crime of the 'enemy of the people', they would hoist your corpse to the highest pinnacle—the crowning insult of tragic derision in the writer's destiny!

And that is not just the fruit of my imagination. In the summer of 1990, the Spanish journalist Elvira Huebles wrote in *El Mundo*, 'In Tirana, one evening in the street, people whom I didn't even know told me that if Ismail Kadare didn't stop criticizing the government, a plot to assassinate him would be carried out.'

The history of 1982 and 1983 was repeating itself. Who were those unknown people who spoke to the journalist? Agents of the Sigurimi who were threatening me? Or sympathizers (which is what I'd like to think)? The question remains unanswered.

11

From the beginning of June it was clear that it would be no ordinary summer. It wasn't just the weather, the countryside, the changing colour of the leaves, but something else, something seen on the faces of the young men. Each passing day cast them in shadow, and not in a figurative sense. They were cast in shadow because they wore beards. For the first time on the streets of Albania one could see flourishing beards on the faces of thousands of young men.

The government, somewhat at a loss, investigated the masks that grew ever darker and augured no good. The smile of socialist optimism, frequently seen at meetings and on television, appeared to melt away under a thick layer of hair. Those bearded faces had nothing in common with the new socialist man invoked in song and fable. These faces were foreign, sombre, menacing. One could well imagine the fear of Party officials, and with them police, informers and other pillars of the state. They complained at their meetings, they spoke before Party committees, they grumbled: What does this mean? These are matters of state, why aren't they being dealt with?

The government, as was its habit of late, waited in anticipation. All its attention was directed towards exposing the 'group of intellectuals' that was fomenting all the trouble.

Previously, when suspicion of that kind was expressed, everyone knew beforehand how events would unfold, and the exposure of the group was an absolute certainty. Four or five weeks might go by before the first arrest was made. Then the next week, a second arrest; without waiting for the third, people would shake their heads pensively and say: 'Another group!'

These practices, however, had become less frequent in Albania. Since the previous autumn, after publication of Tozaj's book *The Knives*, Ramiz Alia had anathematized a group of intellectuals, all the while criticizing Foto Çami, Secretary of the Central Committee in charge of propaganda, for not having anticipated their manoeuvres. (Later, Çami was further criticized, until finally Sofo Lazri was appointed Press Director in Çami's place—which strongly suggests that Lazri was the chief instigator of that piece of intrigue.) But more than half a year had gone by without further reference to the group.

From that time on, however, one could count on two things. First, in keeping with tradition, the group was a fabrication, invented according to a clear plan laid out the moment the prophetic suspicion was announced. Second, the group would be exposed; that is, its existence would be made public.

It was generally supposed that the Sigurimi had been feverishly working to bestow a gift upon the dispenser of all things, the Party. It spared no effort to uncover the group, or more accurately, to invent it. People said that the Sigurimi was midwife to several lists: the longest of these named a hundred and fifty people, and the shortest named twelve. Some of the names were well-known: the physicians, Ylli Popa and S. Berisha, who had written courageous newspaper articles; the academician, H. Béqja, who had published a statement saying that government wrongdoing must be publicly condemned; the economist, G. Pashko, who had given an interview—and not a very agreeable one—to *The Voice of America*; the writer, B. Mustafaj,[10] who had criticized the Sigurimi at a meeting; and the Editor-in-Chief, R. Lani, guilty of having published my interview; plus other journalists, filmmakers, actors, economists, jurists, professors and students. Naturally, Tozaj and I appeared on every list, sometimes at the very top.

In accordance with the usual criteria, as in the case of a good dinner, the group looked very much like a 'good group'. It was substantial (well-known people); it was varied (one of the essential qualities demanded of a group—at least three or four areas of society were represented); it was punctured by specialists of a singular type

(Ylli Popa, Enver Hoxha's physician—well, well, those 'men in white'—since the time of poor Stalin there's no mistaking what they're up to!); it was privileged with opportunities for extensive foreign travel (you'd have to be the village idiot not to wonder about shady deals abroad), and so on.

In the third week of June, when the revised edition of my book *Aeschylus* was published in Albania, I was interviewed by a literary journal. In that interview I denounced the surveillance of intellectuals, and the lists of persons scheduled for arrest. As for the people who drew up those lists, I called them filth. That was my last interview in Albania. It took place just when the journalist Elvira Huebles arrived in Tirana, and strangers confided to her in the street that there was to be an attempt on my life.

An oppressive heat slowed the sense of time during the last days of June. The Turkish embassy, whose iron gates were the first to open, faces the headquarters of the Union of Writers and Artists, which allowed us to watch all that was going on there. In the stifling heat and the dust, crowds rushed from the embassy to the Hotel Arberia, where the first Albanian refugees to secure visas were having their last meal before leaving for Istanbul. Families, friends and admirers, sometimes despairing, sometimes joyous, weeping or merely curious, watched those who seemed to be doing the impossible—they were leaving their own country.

The capital, distressed and helpless as ever, was all anxiety and ferment. The crowd milled in one direction and then in another. The police seemed stupefied. Conflicting orders rained down until at last they ceased because no one could carry them out.

Frenzied, eyes dimmed with tears, people choked on their own words. They had stormed the gates of the French embassy. Italy's as well. The Germans say no. That can't be true, the Germans have let in more refugees than other places. That's right, let's head for the Germans!

Others, usually the oldest, asked: Why the hurry, now that the law has been passed? Wait, children, until the government gives you your passports. Why tear your clothes and hurt yourselves on the ironwork?

But the milling crowd reasoned differently. Sure, try to get a passport, you idiot! Go ahead, and you'll come back from the police station with broken ribs.

Little by little we found out what had happened. The law had in fact been officially announced, but the Ministry of the Interior had not yet ratified it. It was enough to make one despair. The impact, the magic, evaporated. Not only did they issue passports with an eyedropper when they did not want to issue any at all, but those who requested them were often dragged into the depths of the building and beaten without further formality.

The crowd was responding appropriately to the stinginess of a government that had been trained to give nothing without delay, a government that gave with both a clenched fist and a cold heart, with bitterness and spite. People spoke of nothing but the uproar. That evening there was a television report on Serbian terrorism in Kosovo, where half the Albanian nation endured suffering of a different kind. It was the redoubling of those wrongs that led people to sigh as they repeated the old saying—hundreds of years old—Woe to this nation!

12

The evening of 2 July we were at Pashko's. At ten o'clock, his cousin phoned and said, 'If you're thinking of taking a walk, don't do it. There's trouble in the streets.'

I called the house where my sister and youngest daughter were staying. They told me they'd heard shooting, but it was off in the distance. Anxiously, we turned to the Yugoslav television channel for news of what was happening in Kosovo. Serbia was throttling Kosovo. It was the day parliament had been dissolved. A day of mourning for the Albanian nation. As if that weren't enough, a tragedy was being staged here too. (Doesn't the Albanian flag carry the device of a two-headed black eagle?) In Tirana, for the first time in forty-six years of communist power, an insurrection had broken out.

Was it a fateful coincidence or had some diabolical hand orchestrated the two events to reflect each other on the same day?

Could there have been someone, somewhere, whose interest might be furthered by that coincidence? Someone who desired at any cost that the attention given to one of these dramas would distract attention from the other, the way an assassin might stir up conflict in one corner of the city in order to massacre his victims quietly in another?

On that day people asked questions like these in the hundreds; in some ways they were even raised in the press. No one gave an answer.

But the mere fact that these questions were being asked suggested—though in a different way, it's true—a kind of answer to other questions which were even more sombre and insidious. Granted that the coincidence was of some interest to one or the other camp, or to both (which seemed most likely), how had the beneficiaries collaborated in the business? How, and on the basis of what secret pact?

Some day, when history clarifies the enigma of 2 July 1990, it will also provide a key to some of those unexplained events that sealed Albania's tragic destiny in the second half of the twentieth century. (I sometimes tell myself, 'May the Lord grant that I not live long enough to know.' We have witnessed so many horrifying things, we've been disillusioned so many times, we can leave some of that to future generations.)

At about one o'clock in the morning, as we were going home, we saw trucks pass by carrying soldiers and units of armed police. Near the centre of town, in the public park that faces our house, the police were patrolling with dogs. The atmosphere was that of a state of siege.

Part of Tirana never closed its eyes that night. Only the next day did we learn the truth about what happened in Skanderberg Street (Embassy Row). All day long, in the quarter which houses the foreign embassies, chaos exploded. Crowds moved this way and that, there were minor skirmishes with the police, there was tension on both sides. In the evening, thousands of young people came and went along Skanderberg Street, and some stood, threatening, along the pavement. The iron gates of the embassy of the Federal Republic of Germany were only a few paces away. In the eyes of those young Albanians, democracy and the attraction of the West, its music, danger and death, had probably never been so close and so entwined with the image of those iron gates.

By nightfall the ferment intensified. About two o'clock, after a final effort by police to disperse the crowd, the *alabak*—the youthful vanguard of the group—stormed the gates. (In Tirana slang, *alabak* means a new kind of youth; it suggests a parasite, an idler, an adventurer and a bum, yet one with a worthy and upright character.) That word, though unjustly applied to all the refugees early on, is nonetheless crucial to any account of what happened that day. That is not just because many among the crowd were in fact *alabak*, and neither is it because in all they were a minority and yet they set the tone for the entire scene; it's because of something much more profound. Until that time the *alabak* had annoyed the city, exasperating people with their horseplay and practical jokes, but they had never attacked the regime. It was the *alabak* whom the Sigurimi tried to manipulate and turn against the intellectuals. But on that day, for the first time, the *alabak* threw themselves into political action. And for the first time the word *alabak*, after passing our lips over and over, underwent a complete transformation, a rectification. Some days later, when the *alabak* were gone, and had left the city in peace, people used that word with a kind of longing, sometimes even with tears in their eyes. Eventually, however, they stopped using it entirely, as if the *alabak* had carried the word away with them.

It was around ten o'clock when the *alabak* had gone into action. The police fired, first in the air and then at the young men. The *alabak* withdrew, but only a few paces, to the pavement. They could see the weapons being reloaded, they could see those already wounded. But they stood their ground. Five minutes later they moved forward again, this time against a hail of bullets. They fought the police right up to the black iron gates, torn, bloodied, never troubling about death. The number of dead is still not known. Nor is the number of the missing. Later, people spoke about the wounded who were finished off in cold blood. They spoke about the execution of those arrested, about bodies buried secretly in the Mountain of Caves near Tirana. Some even claimed that the regime had allowed the opening of the embassy gates in order to explain the 'disappearances'. Other rumours were spread but never confirmed.

13

Like all decisive events, those that took place at the embassies in Tirana, where the dominant tone was tragic, also had elements of the grotesque and tragicomic. Consistent with the regime's new style, orders came, oblique and contradictory. The embassy gates that only yesterday were like the gates of death suddenly were opened to everyone. Then they closed again—only to reopen once more. People asked themselves, what is this? It was beyond belief but it was true.

Not without a touch of jealousy, the *alabak*, who had paid so dearly for having swarmed over the iron grillwork, watched as others crowded through the gates under the watchful, but now smiling, eyes of the police. The people flocked to swell the ranks—former political prisoners, young couples, pregnant women, the unemployed, students, painters, doctors, Gypsies. People to whom the possibility of leaving the country had never before occurred suddenly found themselves caught up and driven by the demon of adventure: We're leaving, come what may!

The embassy of the GDR attracted the greatest flood of people. Next were the French and Italian embassies. Then, in descending order, all the others: Czech, Polish, Greek, Turkish, even the Chinese. The most hated embassy was the Cuban, because it had delivered into the hands of the police the only two refugees who had gone there, two brothers. The contempt felt for Cuba was so great that people began calling its embassy 'Police Section Number Three'. But that wasn't all. The following day, by way of reprisal, a bomb was thrown at the detested embassy.

The Albanian government tried to exploit the bomb attack, to confer upon it the dimensions of an international plot, but no one paid attention.

In fact, the throwing of that bomb must be seen as a mistake, yet to understand the Albanians—even ever so little—one must consider that the arrogance with which they demanded asylum from the embassies is not unrelated to their ancient Code—which, despite socialism's attempt to stamp it out, reveals itself from time to time, usually when one least expects it. According to the Code, the owner of a house is obliged to open the door and grant refuge to anyone who knocks at the door. A refusal to open the door would be severely punished. So the old formula, 'Do you welcome friends, O master of the house?', now transformed into, 'Do you welcome friends, O foreign embassy?', was as commanding as ever for the Albanians. That is also why, after their arrival in the West, Albanian refugees gave the impression at first of being 'refugees of a peculiar kind'. They were neither obsequious nor grateful; on the contrary, they were rather arrogant and capricious, as the French press in particular remarked. But that was because it seemed to them that in showing hospitality, France, the GDR and all the other countries were simply fulfilling their moral duty, and like friends who had knocked at a door one dark night, these refugees ought to be the object of great respect; and the Marlboro cigarettes that French journalists reproached them for demanding were the least they might expect!

There's no question that this encounter was just one more misunderstanding, added to other tragic misunderstandings which, from age to age, have confronted the Albanian people.

As in the theatre of ancient times, the drama of 2 July was followed by a satirical play before the curtain finally dropped in mourning.

The embassy courtyards, particularly those of Germany, Italy and France, were filled to bursting. Since it was not difficult to enter, there were numbers of people who, once inside, would change their minds for various reasons. Because somebody had told them it was better at the German embassy, or because they hadn't found their friends or the girl they were looking for, not to mention plain curiosity, they would leave their place and go to another embassy. Then they'd have second thoughts, and return to the place they had left, with news about what was happening outside—namely, in the courtyards of other embassies.

Others spent the night at home and returned the next day to claim their 'extraterritoriality'. Still others went off on errands, hoping to buy dollars or to say farewell to relatives. Outside the iron fences, old men and women begged their children to come back, they wept, brought them clothing, shoes, *burek.** From time to time you'd see one or other of them turn and go back, but most responded with mocking gestures to their parents.

A dull anxiety gripped the families of Tirana. Heartsick, parents waited for their children to come home. They tried to guess what the youths were up to in order to avert trouble, but often, when they were feeling more or less assured that their child was only late for dinner, an hour, two hours, and someone would come to tell them, 'He went to the embassy.'

It was quite like living in Ionesco's play, *The Rhinoceros*.

During this time, linguistic and other conventions were changing in the embassy courtyards. People began saying 'Sir,' 'Madam,' 'Miss'; someone baptized a child, nearly everyone wore a cross. As usual in situations of that kind, people told funny stories, like the one about the country bumpkin, just off the train in Tirana, who was looking for an embassy so he could leave the country. He found himself in front of a double-doored portal that was so imposing he thought, 'This surely must be the best embassy.' As soon as he had cleared the entrance he called out to the officer on duty, who waved him away, 'That no longer concerns you. I'm in a foreign embassy now!' At that the officer replied, 'What embassy, you idiot? This is the Ministry of Culture! Now get out of my sight before I lose my temper!' (Two weeks earlier, the would-be émigré would have been taken to the police station in handcuffs, then given ten years imprisonment for attempted escape. Now Party veterans nostalgic for

---

* A meat or vegetable pie.

the good days muttered, *O tempora, o mores.*

For those veteran dogmatists there was indeed a lot to think about. The blood spilt on 2 July wasn't enough for them. They complained that the government hadn't struck a more decisive blow, that the President was waffling. (Oh, why isn't *he* here now? *He* didn't fool around!)

To keep the balance equal, to offset the authorization that had permitted the refugees to leave, to demonstrate that the Albanian government had not yielded to pressure at home or abroad, the regime shook its clenched fist again. Police brutality reached an unprecedented level. People were questioned in the streets, beaten and arrested, sometimes for no reason, sometimes simply because their clothing or their demeanour suggested they were 'that sort'. The police singled out men with beards, even men who hadn't shaved for a day or two; the dictatorship showed once again how thin-skinned it was about whiskers. (Couldn't you see from the start that those beards were bad news? How have we managed to miss what was going on? How could we let them do as they liked for so long? Now we have to hit them where it hurts, and make up for lost time!)

At that juncture, in a fever of unprecedented diplomatic activity, the various foreign governments, the United Nations, the International Red Cross, and Pérez de Cuellar himself tried to resolve the quite urgent problems of the refugees' departure. What they forgot once more was that farce is the second panel of the triptych. The day, or rather, the night that the refugees departed came sooner than anyone had guessed.

It had been a sleepless night in Tirana. More than five thousand people fled the tiny capital. It was as if twenty thousand young refugees were to leave Paris, or two hundred thousand leave Moscow. Night fell on the city. What didn't they say? What didn't they whisper? It was known that the refugees would leave by train and then embark on ships in the harbour at Durrës, but no one knew when. Everyone assumed they would leave that very night, but no one knew when the buses would arrive at the train station—or even which roads they'd take to get there.

Until midnight and even later, the silent crowds moved about blindly, to Durrës Street, to Kavaja Street, to the Grand Boulevard, hoping to catch sight of the buses.

They came around one o'clock in the morning, sombre and silent as hearses (a United Nations representative kept order so that there was neither shouting nor confusion). All one could hear was the noise of the engines. And when the trains actually left for Durrës, a few voices were raised and there were some cries, but it was later, as the refugees began boarding the ships, that people began to sob. In the dark, those who were leaving kissed the ground. Then they walked to where their country ended and the sea began.

In the morning, a little before dawn, people discovered, in the wake of the buses, slips of paper with scribbled addresses and phone numbers, envelopes with photos inside, a bit of money or a keepsake. On most of them, next to the address and phone number, there was a note for whomever might pick up the paper: Dear Friend, please give this message to my mother.

Though written by many hands, they were all in the same style, like the inscriptions on gravestones.

What occurred on the following day was more hateful than the profanation of a grave, more ferocious than a massacre.

It was a rally.

A rally organized by the Party.

To rejoice in the flight of five thousand young Albanians.

To applaud the funeral.

To show the Albanians that the Party was stronger than the nation, that not only could it scoff at blood ties, but it could force the country to celebrate the violation.

From Skanderberg Square to the colonnades of the Palace of Culture, in the presence of a hundred thousand people forced to attend the rally, there appeared the Prime Minister, looking more frail than usual, the Secretary of the Tirana Party Committee, the 'Party Fool', Pirro Kondi, and at the end of the line the official who, according to the radio report, had returned from the mountains to assume the number two position in the government—he was already number one for cruelty. He was Xhelil Gjoni, from the family of Hysni Kapo, and in the eyes of many people his presence meant that dark clouds were gathering over Albania. Behind that group were other members of the government, veterans, representatives of the youth movement, women, workers, philosophers and writers.[11]

Following the customary rites, the dictatorship, once the crime had been committed, proceeded to spread its burden: like the ashes of Vesuvius, the crime must fall on the shoulders of as many people as possible, preferably on everyone's shoulders—which, in a certain sense, might be regarded as justified. At least it showed how barbaric that rally was, perhaps the one most stamped with inhumanity of any ever held in Albania.

The Party imagined that the sinister ceremony (one of the cruellest aspects of tyranny, and especially communist tyranny, is that it has always found a way to associate itself with festive occasions: parades, rallies, processions, festivals, Olympiad) would achieve the breaking of the people. Something *was* broken in Skanderberg Square that day—but it wasn't what the communist government had expected.

The Albanians, accustomed now to call a time of mourning a holiday, and a holiday a time of mourning (hadn't people celebrated in Belgrade with champagne the night that Kosovo wept for its dead?), managed to swallow the indignity. But it was certain to be the last one.

14

That the ugly meeting did not achieve its objective is amply shown by what happened in the small town of Kavaja. That little village, which has a population of thirty thousand and is nowhere mentioned in the history of Albania, suddenly became a bastion of opposition to the government. Disquieting news came from there day and night.

Officials in Tirana didn't dare to drive through the town. It was clear that if Kavaja wasn't given a good lesson, the trouble would spread.

The Sigurimi was confident that it could put down that peaceful market town. Its plan, however, remains a mystery. Something went wrong and they gave it up, but what they managed to accomplish at the outset is enough for us to imagine the horror it was meant to be. A massacre, no doubt. You could see it coming a mile away.

Here's how the attack began: two truckloads of *sampists* tear off like madmen from a village in the Durrës district. They halt at the square in Golemi, between Durrës and Kavaja, where the people of Kavaja go to swim. The *sampists* hurl themselves on the beach like lunatics, beat the bathers and slash the women's bathing suits, insulting and offending them. Before their victims know what has happened to them, the *sampists* climb back into their trucks and take off at full speed for Kavaja. They pour through the streets, yelling, 'We are the sons of Enver Hoxha!' They storm into cafés, insulting and beating people. 'Where have all the brave men of Kavaja gone?' They kill a young man just outside his house . . .

It's the classic scenario of provocation before a massacre.

Kavaja takes up the challenge. Infuriated, the people throw

themselves at the detested *sampists*, they beat and maul them until they disappear from the face of the earth.

But the wrath of the people (as anticipated in the tactics of the massacre) doesn't abate. They attack the buildings of the Sigurimi, of the police, of the Party committee, they break shop windows. It's a typical scene of counterrevolution. After which the use of tanks would seem fully justifiable. And in the wake, there is carnage. Later, inventing the plot is child's play: there's an internal enemy, there are illicit foreign contacts (hasn't everyone seen the cars of foreign diplomats in Kavaja lately?), there's the connection with the refugees leaving, and of course there's the 'group of intellectuals', hand in hand with the CIA, NATO, etc—'just as Comrade Enver taught us long ago.'

How did it happen that this scenario didn't reach its consummation? Why didn't it work? Did someone draw back in fright at the threatened tragedy?

Later, hundreds of people searched for the truth in this affair, but the truth seemed lost in darkness. No one could point out the person who had planned the massacre, nor the person who had prevented it from happening. But one thing had occurred that had never been seen before. The whole town, including the dissidents, the communists, the administrative and legislative bodies, had come together as a unified bloc of opposition.

The national government retreated. The Party leader in Durrës, the detested Muho Asllani—whose jurisdiction extended to Kavaja—was relieved of his duties. And so was the detested leader of the Sigurimi, Zylyftar Ramizi. And then the Director-General of the Police, Dilaver Bengasi. And then the Minister of the Interior, Simon Stefani himself. When Rita Marko was dismissed from the Politburo, my friend Tozaj phoned. 'That makes six. The only one left is the Attorney General.'

But our satisfaction was much diminished; we didn't have the heart to rejoice. Those dismissals, which we otherwise would have cheered joyously, and would have celebrated by inviting one another to dinner and drinking toasts to democracy, had scarcely any effect on us. And it wasn't just us; it was everyone.

It already was *too late*. Too late for everything. Those very words now seemed to belong to the same family as the word 'death'.

Ramiz Alia had lost the historic opportunity. The great door that had been open before him had shut fast, as in Kafka's *The Trial*. Perhaps another door would open to him, a side door. It's true that the doors of history, even the side doors, are not to be neglected.

At the seaside where we were spending the weekend, I asked my oldest daughter to take a walk with me. She was there on vacation and would be going abroad again to pursue her studies. Making the most of the noise of the waves, I told her of my decision to leave. At first I had thought that I shouldn't trouble her prematurely, but on reflection it seemed to me that it would be better if she knew. That way she would be able to say farewell to all the people whom she'd be leaving.

She listened to me and said nothing. But her eyes filled with tears.

15

The summer was coming to an end. It was the time when students returned to school in the capital. We awaited their return with a measure of trepidation since, due to the holidays, they had not taken part in the drama of the summer, and we couldn't know what their reaction would be. The Party committees, more impenetrable than the clouds in the sky, were preparing for autumn. The special envoys returning from conferences, the instructors, the militants, the police spies—all vanished behind closed doors. They came out again, their faces stamped with the troubles of government, to go to other meetings, to the courts, or to their observation posts.

The veil of time was falling upon the events we had just lived through. The details had faded, throwing the essential acts into bold relief. The heroes of the drama could be seen more clearly: those who had confronted the police or the *sampists*, those who had fled the country, those who had been arrested by the Sigurimi and put in prison. But now at the beginning of September, like a far-off reflection of events, hazy as if in a dream, another group of people appeared—those who had taken refuge inside the embassies and then, for one reason or another, had left again, without a word to anyone and without ever returning. ('In our class there are four boys who people think have gone *over there*,' my high-school daughter told me one day. 'They look bewildered. You'd think they have no head on their shoulders, that they've been changed.')

They were indeed another species of humanity. They had gone to the embassy, they had tasted the forbidden fruit in the dens of sin, at the dance of the vampires. Once again they moved among their own people, but their spirits were still marked with the signs of *over there*. ('Everyone looks at them with curiosity,' my daughter tells me, 'as if they were from another planet.')

It wasn't hard to detect the admiration in her voice.

The days jostled one against the other in sterile confusion and agitation.

From time to time voices were heard clamouring for indictments against those responsible (the 'group of intellectuals', etc), but they had no strength of purpose. Everyone was weary.

As time passed, everything that had happened was revealed in all its horror. People had been murdered simply for demanding what they had been promised. They had been insulted, thrown into prison, and shamefully beaten. These were Albanians being killed and beaten by Albanians, in their own country. And it had happened right at the height of our dreams and illusions. I had believed in those illusions with all of my soul. Through my authority as a famous writer I had made those illusions seem plausible. I could not escape remorse.

As for the government, it showed not the slightest intention to offer excuses. To ask pardon, to have pity, is unheard of in the communist world. One of its first aims is to make pity vanish. It is a consequence of Marx's cold heart, of Lenin's narrow spirit, and of all the cruelties and complexes of their successors.

When, in September, at a meeting between the President and a group of intellectuals, I gave my views on the subject, explicitly declaring that official Albania understood neither pity nor pardon, two of the most noble values of humankind, there were many people who said, 'Kadare is raising questions that are completely without merit. What is all this business about asking pardon?' Their brains, dried up by Marxism-Leninism, could not understand that 'this business about asking pardon' is a keystone of every society.

But, though it never occurred to them to ask pardon of the Albanian people for what had happened, the Albanian government was obsessed with ensuring that people who'd either been thrown out of office or demoted would not bear a grudge. They bought Rita

Marko a brand-new Mercedes. They sent the former President of the Supreme Court, whose conscience was burdened with many crimes, to represent Albania at a human rights conference!

The weather turned cold. On the Mountain of Caves people searched for missing bodies. At my desk, I was putting my manuscripts in order. Those that would be published in the next two years. Those whose turn would follow. And then those two hundred pages that would be published only in exceptional circumstances and, probably, wouldn't be published at all since I had taken an oath to burn them if democracy ever came to Albania. It was a promise I had made to the gods, not only out of superstition, but because I believed that democracy was the best thing that could happen to my country.

Meanwhile the rainy season began, and the wet iron gates of the foreign embassies looked blacker than ever. People were gripped by intense emotion as they walked by. Memories came flooding back. *They* had thrown themselves at the iron bars, *they* had been torn and killed. Old women searched days for any trace of them, a shoe or maybe a cap. If they did find something, they'd clasp it to their breast, each believing it had belonged to their daughter or son.

16

I was busy with my manuscripts when my wife came home with a copy of my latest book, *Invitation to the Writer's Studio*, which had not yet been released.

'I managed to get this copy from the printer,' she said. 'But what have you done? You've announced your departure, and openly at that!'

She turned the pages to find the poem, *Time is Too Short*. It was the latest poem I had written, and had been added to the manuscript at the last minute, the day before it went to the printer.

We read it over slowly. She was right. The poem was more than a surprise, and I was astonished at having been so foolish.

In those verses I imagined my last moments, just before death. Suddenly, the grave I was approaching turned into a aeroplane:

Like the traveller and his excess baggage
Near the aeroplane which soon will leave
Heavy laden still
Draw closer to my grave . . .

It was all there: too many bags, without doubt those I was taking as well as those I would leave behind, and that I already missed.

Where to drop this weight, and how?
How to carry this burden?
I cannot drop it down here,
I cannot leave it aloft.

Going down to the grave and going up in a plane, in other words, departing this world and departing Albania, are one and the same. And here is the final stanza:

Tormented to the last instant
By things left unsaid, tragic regret,
I shall give a sign to all
Perhaps unclear, and then I'll go away.

At the bottom of the page were the words, 'Spring 1990'.

Everything was clear. Without meaning to, I'd revealed what I had called my great secret. It wasn't enough that my book *Aeschylus* had ended with the author's exodus; now I'd made this cry as well.

I said to Elena, 'What can I do? Now it's written like an announced departure!'

But I wasn't sorry, because a kind of superstition had always led me to believe that the trouble a poem can bring you is usually less serious than other troubles.

My publisher, Claude Durand,[*] whom I had asked to visit me, arrived with his wife on 11 September.

After he'd had dinner with us at home, I told him what I intended to do while accompanying him back to the Hotel Dajti. He listened calmly. No more than Michel Piccoli had he ever encouraged me in that direction.

Like the true friend he is, he spoke of the difficulties that might arise, but he did so without ever questioning my plans. The next day we went out to walk and to speak quietly on a deserted beach, near Durrës. As we walked along the wet sand, I told him, 'Last night, collapsing on the bed, I wished with all my might that the sun would never rise again.'

'I understand completely,' he said.

The next day, 13 September, I accompanied him and his wife to the airport. They were taking with them my youngest daughter, who

---

[*] Librairie Arthème Fayard, Paris.

didn't yet know anything about our own departure. Elena and I had reserved our tickets for 27 September. The airport personnel let me walk out to the runway with Claude and his wife, and I told him once more what I had already said: 'If our daughter's presence in France would mean that we cannot go there, you must send her back to us at once. Then I will be forced to leave her' (at the last second I swallowed the words, 'to be sacrificed') . . . 'here'.

He nodded—a special nod, serious, one that I was familiar with—and we parted.

Two weeks later, on 27 September, we left in turn. Elena had taken a tranquillizer. I was close to prostration.

We said very little.

As the plane flew over northern Italy, we agreed that it might be good to make a retreat for some time in a monastery.

The plane had already reached the skies of France. No doubt that's when it struck me that this journey, for me, was really a journey to prison. Since I hadn't managed to be imprisoned in Albania, I had come to be in my own prison in France.

France, November 1990

PART TWO

Letters

The letters published in this section are not merely useful for understanding the chain of events and how they came about; they also help to understand something more important. That is, they show in what manner and at what pace the minds of the people of that part of the world were changing in that memorable year.

The thawing of people's minds, after more than forty years, is a painful process to which all people of the communist world, in varying degrees, have been subjected, from the most humble to Heads of State. Let us not forget that it is to the liberation of man from his masters that we have dedicated one of our most sublime myths: the myth of Prometheus.

These letters are not testimony served up as a curiosity, nor are they framed as an indictment. They are, above all, messages of hope and faith in the evolution and emancipation of mankind.

Letter from Ismail Kadare to Ramiz Alia (3 May 1990)

Comrade Ramiz,

A Canadian of Lebanese origin, Mr Mehlem Mobarak, has asked me to give you a book which he wanted you to be aware of. It's a shameful work by V. Georgevitch, *The Albanians and the Great Powers*, in which there is an autograph dedication by Prince Kara Georgevitch: 'I hope to see you soon in Albania where I am now convinced that we shall go and stay.'

Mr Mobarak has also informed me that he has roughly eight hundred volumes and various important documents concerning Albania, which he would like to present as a gift to our country.

I take advantage of the occasion to express my pleasure, and that of all intellectuals, in the decisions of the Ninth and Tenth Plenary Sessions, and especially in your own decisions concerning the democratization of our country's economy, society and foreign policy.

All upright intellectuals, and indeed all Albanians who love their country, support without reservations your efforts to improve the welfare of our people and to democratize public life in Albania. These are events of historic significance, and they can only grow in importance over the years to come.

For that very reason—and for that reason alone—allow me to express certain thoughts and anxieties that have come to me as a citizen and as a writer, and that I believe are shared by many others.

If the overwhelming majority of the Albanian people has greeted with enthusiasm these first steps towards democracy, and even hungers for more, a handful of people are against it and will oppose our efforts to their dying day. The array of these hostile forces is most significant.

In the front ranks are the sworn enemies of this country, like Arshi Pipa,[1] who has declared, for example, that re-establishing relations with the United States was a bad undertaking.

In addition, the chauvinist Serbs, after hearing of these steps towards a democratic programme and of the new directions in Albanian foreign policy, greeted it as a day of mourning.

Finally, as paradoxical as this may seem, the dogmatic and conservative circles in Albania, careful to defend their own narrow interests, are adamantly opposed to change. Their attitude is paradoxical indeed, since they proclaim themselves guardians of moderation; narrow-minded as they are, they know perfectly well that their position coincides with that of Albania's enemies, yet they persist and sign. That just goes to show their bad faith; it's the reason they've lost their last chance, which was to be regarded as imbeciles. More and more they act to deliberately interfere with the development of democracy.

At the moment these groups are attempting, if not to form a coalition, at least to act in concert, moved by the instinct of self-preservation: they try to take advantage of the weaknesses and the worries that the process of democratization begets, and everyone knows how difficult that process is, riddled with pitfalls.

Democracy is a beautiful word, but the road that leads to it is by no means easy. On the contrary, it is one of the most difficult paths that a country can choose. But, like all roads that lead to freedom, it is also, for the peoples of this world, the road to greatness and security. All others lead sooner or later to the abyss.

In Albania today, openly or indirectly, the forces of reaction are attempting, and will continue attempting, to restrain that vital impulse. They exploit the outbreaks prompted by that impulse, they exaggerate them, as at this moment when they turn to provocations, leading people astray or heightening their exasperation.

I have no pseudo-intellectual obsessions with regard to the Ministry of the Interior or to the Police. For me, as for all real intellectuals, that attitude of affected scorn for the police, which for some is an automatic reaction, is quite foreign. I sincerely admire those officials of the Ministry of the Interior, the inspectors and police who, on duty all night long, honestly work to defend the interests of the citizens and the state of Albania. It is not the truncheon—in some people's minds, the very symbol of dictatorship—that troubles me any more than the rigour of the police when it comes to hard cases, the street rabble, bandits, thieves and criminals. After all, the least one can say is that the police have not always shown the severity towards such people that perhaps they should.

No, something else is troubling me: the zeal and the psychosis which has been spreading lately inside the Ministry of the Interior. It's a matter of bitter reality, but I think that, as Head of State of a small but not insignificant country, you must know the truth. Because if appropriate measures are not taken, that zeal, that immoral enthusiasm that promises no good, will have dreadful consequences.

Recently in the Ministry of the Interior, certain high officials have persuaded themselves, before they persuaded others, that they are the sole guarantors of the government's stability, and that because the regime would crumble without their presence, they are the repository of hope and safety.

It stands to reason that, in order to strengthen that feeling, the information they give you must be selectively chosen and carefully framed. Warping the truth is not difficult, any more than sowing panic by drawing false or biased conclusions.

The great majority of Albanians who show their rage here at home do so not because they are demanding the return to power of the Turkish beys or the great landowners but, on the contrary, because they see their phantoms reincarnated in the government bodies of today.

There are many reasons for their exasperation: the economic situation, housing conditions, the problems of daily life, etc. But the most intolerable, in their eyes, is the violation of the rights of man: beatings, arbitrary arrests, threats and humiliations of all sorts. Well, the Ministry of the Interior seems not to understand that these abuses, which we had just about managed to guarantee people against, became absolutely intolerable during the events we all know about, and to let these things continue will only bring tragedy.

The various organs of the dictatorship are straining every nerve to legitimize these abuses, so as to have a free hand and to go further still. They have not hesitated to spread the word everywhere: 'Ramiz Alia has authorized us to take that kind of action.'

All Albania knows about the beating perpetrated in the Dega building* and by the police; you will probably learn of these abuses only with great difficulty, and even then will be given a watered-down version of the facts, since those whose proper job is to inform you have no interest in putting those things before you as they really happened. They think that by threatening the victims of cruel abuse and by forcing them to remain silent, they will put a stop to the spread of the truth on this subject. But now the truth can be heard everywhere in the streets. And the truth is horrifying.

In my post as Vice-President of the Albanian Democratic Front, I received many, many complaints from citizens whose personal rights have been flagrantly violated.

I will only mention a few instances here, concerning people engaged in the arts: Hektor Pustina and Reiz Çiço, both assistants at the Kinostudio, and Yeli Beqiraj, a painter, were beaten and otherwise abused at the Dega without having been charged with any wrongdoing. They divulged these things during a public meeting of the Tirana Party Committee, but their complaint has never been answered. Not only did they receive no apology, but they continue to be classed as hooligans.

When Fatmei Musaj, a painter from Kavaja, protested at the brutal treatment of his brother, a musician, he was ordered to the Dega, where he was insulted and then threatened so as to ensure his silence.

Illir Adili, an economist in Tirana, was arbitrarily arrested and held for thirty-six hours, during which time he was threatened and

---

* A local post of the Sigurimi.

beaten, and was subjected to both physical and psychological violence.

I shall not add further to this list of the abused. But I shall mention one last case. In the course of the interrogation of Illir Adili, among the many hysterical insults heaped upon him by officials of the Dega in Tirana, there was one in particular addressed to the 'writers and intellectuals of the Kadare stamp who want to sell Albania to American imperialism.'

These insults came from two Sigurimi agents, Hodo Hodaj and Gezim Bejko.

Although I have no particular obsessions about the Ministry of the Interior, it goes without saying that I have no particular esteem for it either; for years now I have been aware of their feelings about me, in which ill will and plain foolishness rival each other. That's why, even though the Ministry has been opening my mail regularly for more than twenty years, it has never disturbed me in the least. It troubles me so little that at the time of our recent conversation, in which I mentioned several delicate matters, I made no mention of it. I am sufficiently abreast of what is happening to know that opening mail and tapping phone conversations is only one step away from complete surveillance. However, that too has never really troubled me, not because I am particularly brave, but because I can distinguish between certain mechanisms of government and the government itself, and I am not unaware that the machinery of any government, however free it may be, harbours a certain element of the absurd.

To return to the two members of the Sigurimi, it's not so much the fact that they mentioned my name that I find disturbing—I'm used to that!—but it's the general psychosis which has developed against the intelligentsia from within the depths of the Ministry of the Interior.

I am convinced that in this instance the word *intelligentsia* is simply a euphemism behind which contempt for the democratic position taken by the Ninth and Tenth Plenary Sessions is hidden. From hatred of the intelligentsia to hatred of the democratic orientation of those plenums, and of your own declarations, there is in fact only a short step.

I am not acquainted with the Vice-Minister of the Interior, Zylyftar Ramizi,[2] whom I understand from everyone is very bad news. Are we to imagine that the Albanian people have lost all political and common sense, to the point of making idle accusations—meaning that they would like or hate someone for no good reason? I think our people still have a great deal of sense. They know very well what they like and what they do not like.

It is notorious in Albania that Zylyftar Ramizi personally takes part, with remarkable zeal, in the beating of people detained, that he is the primary instigator of the mad psychosis I have mentioned, and that he is the person responsible for the hatred that has arisen among our people.

I know quite well the Director-General of the Police, Dilaver Bengasi, who has just completed and brought to your attention a study entitled *The Use of Police Forces in Dispersing Crowds*. I have always been astonished that this not very gifted imposter has had such a brilliant career and was given a rather delicate mission to accomplish, at the time he tried to institute a lawsuit against me during the days when he was public prosecutor in Tirana.

Hatred of the intellectuals seems to drive the two people whom I have just mentioned. Well, how can they love the people, or their country, when they detest those who represent the nation's culture?

By a bizarre coincidence, Zylyftar Ramizi is Vice-President of the Commission on Law of the People's Assembly, the commission whose business it is to supervise the execution of his own work!

For a long time Spiro Koleka[3] was the official responsible for overseeing the application of laws in the Presidium of the People's Assembly. At the time I was a member of that body, and I remember that when it came to upholding human rights, not only would he do nothing of the kind but he would go directly counter to that end. In a sense his position couldn't have been more logical, since his own son, the examining magistrate in the Ministry of the Interior, had a reputation as a sadistic criminal against whom all charges were dismissed.

A perfectly innocent young woman student was beaten with an

iron bar at his instigation. She still lives in Tirana, forever disabled, while that so-called judge has been promoted for 'meritorious service' to the Ministry of Foreign Affairs, where he still works.

Rita Marko,[4] who replaced Spiro Koleka, has, like his predecessor, not the least notion of the law. That is one of the reasons why the people want no more of that wretched crew. Those ministers, knowing that the people reject them, are full of hatred for the people, and have turned against them, denouncing them for their lack of gratitude, etc, and promulgating decrees which allow them to imprison all those who dare to criticize them.

I am distressed at having to write these bitter words. But you have opened new horizons to the Albanian people, and if you do not want them to be downcast, to weaken, to close themselves up again, then we have a duty, as citizens of this country and in the name of those new horizons, to give you our help and our support.

There are people who will struggle against democratization, and who have already banded together with a single sordid objective: to keep their privileged positions. For, as in every truly progressive movement, democratizing the social structure threatens the comfort and grateful torpor of those in office.

Everybody talks about those privileges, but I am convinced, in this matter too, that the information you receive and the manner in which it is expressed is quite altered. Setting aside those who have a mania for criticism, there is no serious person in all of Albania who doesn't understand and doesn't think it reasonable that the Head of State and certain highly placed ministers, just as in other countries, live under quite special conditions. Those conditions, in most cases, are adopted for security reasons, and are as much privations as they are privileges.

When the people grumble about privileges, they are certainly not talking about the conditions I have mentioned. They are protesting most loudly against unjustified privilege, abuses, attacks on the basic foundation of our Constitution: the equality of the citizens. In plain language, the people rise up against the situation enjoyed by a good number of families who, in accordance with an old tradition, hold on to privilege when there is nothing to justify it. These families bring in their train a swarm of distant relatives—cousins male and female, uncles and aunts, daughters-in-law and sons-in-law who not only are dissatisfied with their unearned privileges (special food supplies, vacations in places reserved for them and well policed, etc) but think it appropriate to boast, which never fails to stir the people to legitimate anger.

Those who have any understanding of human nature, and particularly the Balkan temperament, will understand how a permanent challenge of that kind can become intolerable, *a fortiori* in a socialist country where property is supposed to be collective.

I'm convinced that the echoes of that revolt must have reached you in a distorted form, badly interpreted, and presented as an attempt to overthrow the government. That conclusion is wonderfully suited to the aims of the reactionary forces.

Those forces will stop at nothing to sabotage the development of democracy: they will provoke the wrath of the people and bring about disorder so they can say, 'That's where democratization leads us. That's where the conclusions of the Ninth and Tenth Plenary Assemblies lead us.' The classic method.

To preserve their own interests, those people will stop at nothing to demonstrate that socialism cannot be sustained without violence, and on this point as on so many others, their position coincides perfectly with that of the enemies of socialism. To them, socialism and democracy are incompatible ideals, each excluding the other. And to them, socialism means privilege, violation of the law, abuses, ignorance and lethargy.

When people of that ilk appear in public, they enrage the citizens. The hollow speeches, the crude threats uttered by some of them bore one to death, and as soon as the news reaches the people, that feeling turns to animosity.

At the last Plenary Session of the Central Committee of the Youth Movement, the President of the Supreme Court, Aranit Çela, speaking of the democratization of the legal arsenal, was unable to hide his anxiety about the reforms, and he showed it quite clearly in this threat: 'Even today, whoever attempts to escape will leave his bones on the frontier!' Can a magistrate who is also a President of the Supreme Court use such language as this?

There are many people who would like to know, and with good reason, how it happens that the 'experts' concerned with democratization of the judicial arsenal are the very people responsible for violating the law.

By way of example, I name the President of the Supreme Court, and also the Attorney General, Rapi Mino, who for long years were enthusiastic collaborators with the Minister of the Interior, the minister whom we are told was director at that time of 'a nest of serpents' run by criminals like Kadri Hazbiu and Feçor Shehu.[5]

You know better than anyone else how that evil legislation brought irremediable damage to our socialist government in the minds of the Albanian people, and even more in international opinion. Today the forces of reaction want at all costs to sustain and preserve that bad seed. They claim that they are acting for the good of the country, and of socialism, while in fact the good is negligible when balanced against the evil that comes of it. For if, after the current session of the People's Assembly, Albania is still endowed with anachronistic laws which are not in force in any other European country, her bad reputation will be heightened still more, and many important things will be sadly compromised. But the effect would be gripping indeed if Albania demonstrated to the rest of the world that socialism could come to be democratic. Nothing could be more crushing than if the opposite were to happen.

Incoherence, a kind of indulgence for bad conduct, and even more the satisfaction with which it is sometimes greeted, counteract the healthy climate brought about by the Ninth and Tenth Plenary Assemblies. I cannot see what advantage our country can gain by those absolutely unjustifiable killings perpetrated on our borders, as in the recent case of the couple in Shkodra who were surrounded and murdered for no reason at all. That double murder, committed just when the new law authorizing freedom to travel abroad is under discussion, has stunned popular opinion in Albania; investigating and condemning the guilty would be much more suitable than the cynical pleasure expressed here and there by the partisans of violence: 'Serves them right! That's what I call a job well done!'

The citizens of a sovereign nation may not be dragged through the mud, arbitrarily arrested, humiliated, and beaten—even less shot down like dogs.

I hate to trouble you with the sombre paragraphs of this letter, but today I read your speech in Kolonje in which you say you want the truth about what is happening in this country; that is why I resolved to set these things down.

As I mentioned earlier, the road to democracy is arduous indeed. There will be excesses, misunderstandings, difficulties, mad words and actions, abuses. All this can be expected. That is the nature of that road. For the same reason it has grandeur, even heroism. If you choose to take that path, history will applaud you for your great worth. The worth of a man who, at a favourable moment in history, was willing to choose the right road, the only one to pursue.

Despite the difficulties, that road follows its own logic, which is an uninterrupted journey forward: to press on with firm steps, like the people of our rugged mountains, but above all never stopping and never turning back. In the destiny of peoples, nothing is more bitter than hope deceived. It is the source of violent change and catastrophe.

The people are with you. A handful of blind factions bent on counteracting the course of democracy do not amount to much when seven million Albanians hope that the future of this country will be unmistakably its proper future. When those factions have been relegated to the rubbish heap by the forces of history, they will be recognized for what they are, laughable and ridiculous. In that joyous time people will feel a tiny scruple of regret: How much importance we attributed to them! How much we overestimated them! How much energy we spent in vain!

The people of Albania are with you because the future lies with you. That people understands things very well, and when it comes to basic things, their understanding is infallible. Even as they will answer neglect with indifference, so will they keep always in memory and in their heart those who have loved them, those who have toiled for them, not in arousing their wrath or crushing them, but in working for their well-being, their happiness, and their freedom. That destiny is yours. The future lies in you. Albania is with you.

Respectfully,

Ismail Kadare
Tirana, 3 May 1990

Ramiz Alia's Reply to Ismail Kadare
(21 May 1990)

Dear Ismail,

I have your letter of 3 May 1990. Since I have been very busy, it has been impossible for me to answer sooner. Not that you were expecting an answer, but because I have some things to say to you. I have always spoken frankly to you. I shall do that now.

Your letter did not make a good impression on me, and not because of its 'sombre' paragraphs, but because of your rancorous explosion at what you regard as reactionary forces, and for the fulsome praise that you direct to me personally. Make no mistake about it: I protect no retrograde forces, whatever the wrappings they may show, just as I can pride myself on never hiding any violation of the law on the part of police officers or any other organs of the state. Our government has never hesitated, nor shall it ever hesitate, to condemn any official wrongdoing.

In regard to the cases you mention in your letter, I have ordered that an investigation be made. But when you bring up these matters, the fact that your preoccupations are concentrated solely on conservative circles—while you are silent about the forces of reaction that, whether abroad or within our borders, are trying to incite us to give up our freedom and independence, as a people and as communists—that fact, I tell you frankly, troubles me. For your conclusion, according to which a current of hostility is developing in the councils of the Ministry of the Interior, is quite unfounded, and what is more, tendentious.

As for the praise that you accord me, do not forget, Comrade Ismail, that every one of our actions is connected with the Party, with its strength and its clear-sightedness. It is the Party that has educated us, the Party that has inspired us, the Party that has given us the courage to meet every storm. I am most grateful for the approbation that comes from the people—I have received a very large number of letters and telegrams from private persons and from groups—just as you have, but personally, I have done nothing special during the Ninth and Tenth Plenary Sessions of the Central Committee of the Party. I do not deserve all those compliments. As happens with every director, I have done no more than to bring together in a speech the ideas expressed by the communists, the workers, the youth movement, the intellectuals, the various specialists, and the peasants. I do not say this out of modesty. I have done no more than to express a truth that has been forged in meeting after meeting by the comrades in the Party and the representatives of diverse social groups.

If I emphasize this point it is not because I want to appear to be 'a man of principle', but because my attention was drawn to the fact that, in your letter of some three thousand words, not once did I find the word 'Party'. Even when you mention the Ninth and Tenth Plenary Assemblies, you do not point out that these are bodies of the Central Committee of the Party. That also struck me in the interview you gave recently to *The Voice of Youth*.[6] Perhaps you were concerned about being overly formal, perhaps it was simply an oversight. But at a time when reactionaries—not conservatives—are preaching with such violence the pure and simple liquidation of the Communist Party, and where, under pressure, they have even come to changing the name of the Party and the various republics, neither such an oversight nor the desire to avoid formality can serve the defence of our independence or our struggle to revolutionize and democratize public life. Without the Party, without socialism, a free and sovereign Albania cannot exist. Consequently, democracy for the people would not exist.

I have read with great attention several interviews given by our comrades to the foreign press. The foreigners are interested solely in questions concerning freedom of expression, the broadcasting of a possible schism within the Party, fidelity or lack of fidelity to the

Albanian Spring

policies of Enver Hoxha, etc. In the answers made by our comrades—which were generally correct—I think it's important that we profit by such occasions to affirm very clearly our socialist policy, to emphasize more explicitly the tone and positions of the Party, instead of keeping silent about its existence. That might possibly look like formalism—but not at this time.

In Albania, just as the struggle for national freedom has been victorious under the Party's direction, so will the current programme to develop the country be achieved only under the same direction. That policy is the sole guarantee that whatever develops will be for the good of the country, the people and socialism. That policy is our sole guarantee that economic growth and cultural progress, the improvement of living conditions, our relations with the rest of the world, and the general emancipation of individuals and society as a whole, can develop as it should.

The Party works in the progressive spirit of our age. In so doing, it comes to grips with economic and social changes as well as with the expanded role of the Albanian citizen. But by what means do we expect to achieve these things? Is it by conforming to the dictates and models of the rest of the world, or is it in following our own convictions, in preserving our sovereignty, our unique identity, and our national traditions?

I believe that every clear-sighted person, every patriot, every communist would prefer the second approach. That is what we have always done. Even our battle, our socialist transformation, our agricultural policy, our policies on education and culture carry the Albanian stamp. That is what marks our unique national character.

In our times, in the West and in the East, reaction aims at imposing its own methods, presenting them as the indispensable condition for being accepted into the international community. In the same way, it involves the market economy and hence the development of private property, and the opening of our country to investment and participation of foreign capital; also plural political parties, and therefore the creation of anti-socialist parties that would bring about the division of our country—quite different from the pluralism of ideas, the encouragement and spread of free discussion,and so on—all these things being presented as universal models.

For us, a small nation surrounded by neighbours who bear us ill will, it's not socialism alone that is in danger, but the freedom and independence of our native land.

I'm sure that you are perfectly familiar with these problems; nevertheless, in your letter you ignore the danger. Foreign pressure does not just threaten a few individuals; it puts a rope around the neck of the entire Albanian nation, so as to overturn the power we bought with our blood, and to restore foreign dominion to this land.

Your works are dedicated to the defence of our native country, to its freedom and independence, as well as to the heroic struggle of our Party and to Comrade Enver Hoxha's efforts to preserve Albania's sovereignty. (I am thinking of *The General of the Dead Army, The Drums of Rain, The Great Winter, What Do the Mountains Think?, Eagles Fly High,* and *The Concert*—which, by the way, I thank you for sending in the French edition, etc.) These books all redound to your honour, not simply as a writer but as a combatant, as a patriot, and as a communist. The people love your work, and the Party has always held your books in high esteem. You must not forget what Comrade Enver Hoxha did for you, nor the marked preference that I have always accorded you. After all, if I write to you in this way, frankly and without diplomacy, that certainly reflects our friendly relations, but just as importantly it reflects the Party's esteem for Ismail Kadare, whom we have wished and still wish will remain not only a great writer but a steady fighter for the Party and the people.

I did not understand your polemic with Arshi Pipa on *The Voice of America*. It was weak and couched defensively. In the typical way that international forces of reaction manoeuvre with respect to Albania, the provocateur Arshi Pipa tried in that interview to make you distance yourself from Enver Hoxha and to renounce your work and activities as a militant. He declared that the fact that Ismail Kadare now expresses himself as a proponent of democracy and human rights, and that he troubles himself to criticize the shortcomings in that area, was not sufficient. Arshi Pipa meant that you must renounce socialism and the system you have defended in your work. He was not, then, offering a literary critique, and couldn't care less if you criticized or praised the government. In my opinion, your defence accordingly should also have been political. It was, to say the least, incongruous to answer Arshi Pipa by saying that in the past he had 'denounced' you and that because your book is a 'literary work', it does not aim to criticize the government or extol the cult of personality. Such a response is too short and lacks force.[7]

Now, your work is certainly an artistic accomplishment, but it carries a well-defined message: it tells of the heroic struggle by the people, the Party, and Enver Hoxha to defend freedom, the independence of our native land, and the socialist ideal. Without that unequivocal message, your work would not have the special value that it does. And it is precisely that message, that hymn to the people and to socialism, that Arshi Pipa cannot bear.

It seems to me that in order to defend that militant message you should have firmly opposed that lackey of reaction, that enemy of socialist Albania. The struggle to democratize Albanian life and the heroic combat of our Party and Enver Hoxha for the defence of freedom, independence and the socialist ideal are indistinguishable.

Today, Comrade Ismail, when the cause of the independence of the country and of socialism is the target of various reactionary forces, when our nation lies threatened as never before in its young history, the people and the Party need more of that militancy and resolution from everyone—from workers and from intellectuals, from the young and from veteran fighters. It is proper and fitting to resist the enemy's attack by using every weapon. We must rally round the Party and support its revolutionary measures in the economic domain as well as in the democratization of society.

No isolated individual, no force—whatever it might be—can accomplish anything without the Party, without following its vibrant course. The Party advances on the right road, intelligently and securely. Its directives in the domain of culture, in social life, and in the life of the government must be carried out. To that end we must stimulate the enthusiasm of the masses, who must find before them a united front of militants, and not people 'with affected scorn' as you call it! (There are too many people to count these days who have that attitude and have learned, or rather learned amiss, the terms 'democracy' and 'worldwide declaration of human rights', which they then employ in their own fashion.) In fighting for measures to democratize the life of the country, no doubt we shall have our hands full. At the same time we must fight against those forces that are opposed to democracy. And they are quite diverse: from right and left, conservatives and dogmatists, liberals and opportunists, the incompetent and the mediocre, careerists and bureaucrats, degenerates and anti-socialists. The battle must be led; it cannot be guided individually, but only in unity, working broadly and extensively, setting the masses on the march by means of Party organizations, mass organizations, the press, television, etc. As we mark the steps along the way towards revolutionizing the country and the Party, steering a path towards democratization and mass participation, we must be most vigilant and act wisely to defend the freedom of our socialist country. Albania must never become Romania, nor Poland, no more than Bulgaria or Yugoslavia. That would bring a curse on future generations, a curse upon our people.

I have written to you most frankly, for I know that you too prefer that things be said without kid gloves. But I am compelled to do so for another reason: I wish that among the people and among our intellectuals, as well as in foreign opinion, people should not see Ismail Kadare as someone who involves himself in criticizing the Sigurimi and the police, the dogmatists and mediocre talents in the arts, but that they see in him a communist writer who, in this difficult period, struggles in unison with the Party to defend the freedom of our native land and the development of socialism in Albania. In that matter, no one should have the slightest doubt.

My best regards,

Ramiz Alia
Tirana, 21 May 1990

To the President of the People's Socialist Republic of Albania (23 October 1990)

My decision to leave our country temporarily was not arrived at lightly. But my conscience is quite clear. Several times, in conversations or in writing, I have expressed openly the essentials of my thoughts. In the letter I addressed to you on 3 May of this year, and particularly during our long discussion last February, I told you without equivocation that the Albanian people have a pressing need for improved economic welfare and for democracy. True democratization of public life, the renunciation of violence, liberation of political prisoners, an end to isolationism and the defence of Stalin, the restoration of religious freedom and freedom of expression: these are some of the imperative needs that I brought to your attention in detail this spring. They are the logical extension of what I have expressed and defended in my writings for a number of years, as is my decision to leave our country. In that regard, I want to make it clear that my work will remain as I wrote it in Albania, without changing or retouching anything; regardless of what my detractors might say, they will bear witness that the values created in that country, even in difficult times, remain incontestable.

Last spring, like the great majority of Albanians and many of the nations of this world, I believed confidently that you would proceed with the democratization of the country, ensuring the gratitude of our people throughout your lifetime. But it appears that hidden forces or some part of your own conscience have led you to do the opposite of what you had promised. And since then, we all know what has come about: police violence, assassinations, and great disappointment.

I decided to leave our country on the day I became convinced that my efforts as an intellectual in helping to bring about a softening of the regime were all in vain. From that time, I could not go on taking part in a parody of democracy, nor contribute to the perpetuation of an illusion.

Last spring you still held all the cards that would permit the beginning of a new era in the history of the Albanian people. But you ran away from that wonderful opportunity. I am still hopeful, nevertheless, that you will seize your last chance to avoid bloodshed. An outcome of that sort would be catastrophic for the Albanian people, within Albania and beyond her frontiers, where our enemies would delight in her discomfiture. History would regard you as immensely worthy were you to avoid such a tragedy.

I hope you will listen to the voice of reason, and it is that hope that led me to say at the outset that I was leaving Albania *temporarily*. If Albania becomes a true democracy, I shall return to my country immediately. I mean to say quite clearly here that I would return not after an overthrow of the regime, but whenever a genuine programme of democratization has begun.

Those people or that part of your own conscience that persuaded you that the democratic current would bring about your overthrow know nothing of the aspirations and political acumen that the experience of a long, dramatic history has bestowed upon the Albanian people.

The Albanians, taken as a whole, including those of Kosovo in Yugoslavia, have never had their eyes as wide open as at the present time. Never again can the Albanian people be deluded by any of those doctrines or theories that have been used until now to justify the poverty and the lack of democracy in which they live. Now the Albanians have become aware that they are one of the oldest peoples of Europe, and that they deserve a better fate. Albania has had every chance of becoming one of the most prosperous and free countries on the continent: not only has she not achieved that, but by a dreadful paradox, as if to complete her tragic history, she has been deliberately severed from the peoples of Europe.

At the time of our conversation last February, when the discussion came to the point of whether or not to give the peasants the right to own cattle, I mentioned to you that in Albania, during the last few years, a terrible accusation had been levelled at the regime: the wilful impoverishment of the population. In the eyes of those who make that accusation, socialism deliberately impoverishes the people in order to dominate them more easily. While challenging that accusation, you agreed, a few days later, to give cattle to the peasants, but you went no further. Nevertheless, the government has been careful not to express any criticism of its absurd conduct, and has not recalled those people who bear a heavy responsibility for that monstrous pro-gramme of enforced misery. The refusal to recognize its mistakes, the complete lack of repentance and compassion, are among the most inhumane traits of a government; and to think that socialism prides itself on being the most humane regime of all!

Wherever Albanians are living in the world, they ask themselves, without exception, what it is that keeps those in power from seeing what is so obvious to ordinary people. If their question is rarely addressed to the many ministers of the state, that is because no one trusts either their abilities or their moral sensitivity. On the contrary, they often raise the question with you in mind. And because it is impossible for them to find any other explanation, the people begin to believe a conjecture which has spread everywhere as a rumour —that there are documents with which you can be blackmailed, so that you have been forced to adopt a policy that has already been set out; in a word, your hands have been tied. Again, according to that hypothesis, the documents in question have been deposited somewhere in Albania, or even in the hands of a hostile foreign power that would like to see the Albanian nation in ruins. Personally, I find that suggestion quite unconvincing, but the fact that it is current reveals remarkably well the irrational and anti-historical aspect of what is happening in Albania. Such nonsense, running against the tide of history, cannot endure.

Because I have written a letter of this nature, and because I have left our country, an unpleasant tradition allows you to call me a traitor, an agent of the international bourgeoisie, etc, but everyone knows that there is nothing to be gained by such falsehoods.

I leave our country with great bitterness. I would give anything so that my departure not be the cause of instability, and even less of disorder and violence. On the contrary, I would wish that the Albanians might finally forget the hatred that has made them suffer so much, that they might hold out their hands to one another in reconciliation, learn tolerance at last, and generosity, and renounce violence and the vengeful spirit that can only beget new crimes. The Albanian people need now more than ever to embark upon a new way of life. But on the eve of that new era they also need more than ever a time of repentance, of spiritual growth, and of purification. However, that purification, that internal harmony, cannot be attained while a large contingent of irresponsible people still hold the reins of power. That band of uncivilized, by turns savage and servile, careerists and illiterates, whose counsel is notoriously anti-Albanian and sadistic, whose brains have atrophied, no longer suit this time and are unworthy of our country. That is why the people are exasperated, that is why they lose patience and live permanently in deep depression. That crushing mortgage continues to enlarge the gulf between the Albanian people and those who lead them.

The refusal to honour the concepts of liberty and the rights of man, the lack of respect for the Albanian nation, and at the opposite pole the unbridled cult of Marxism-Leninism, with its slogans like 'The Albanians will eat grass if necessary to defend Marxism-Leninism,' the defence of Stalin, and above all your absurd and unconstitutional conceptions of the legitimacy of the ruling power are only one feature of that frightful mortgage. When you declare that you are 'ready to defend the regime even if it comes to bloodshed,' do you not see that such a declaration implies a violation of international law and makes its author an outlaw? The people are right to think that the real meaning of that slogan is nothing less than, 'We shall defend our status and our privileges, even if it comes to bloodshed!'

The Albanian nation has the most pressing need to be integrated with Europe. For a long time now the people have understood that she cannot be kept apart, like an orphan, but must ally herself with her European family, in keeping with her own dignity.

You have one more chance to make the difficult transition and to do it in such a way that it comes without pain or bloodshed.

The Albanian people, whether they live within our boundaries or suffer in Kosovo, are living in troubled times. Tragic times, in which the future hangs in the balance. History will pitilessly avenge those who had the power to avoid catastrophe but did not do so.

Ismail Kadare

P.S. I would like to give the Albanian government a chance to demonstrate that it is still capable of tolerance and has the decency to respect Albania's culture. In my apartment in Tirana, which is now occupied by my mother and my sister, are my personal files, my manuscripts, my correspondence, my notes and notebooks. I hope one day to find them intact.

With the money on deposit in my wife's name at the Central Savings Bank of Tirana, that apartment might be bought or continue to be rented, and all the costs thereof paid for a long time. I am returning by cashier's cheque the sum of five hundred dollars given to me by the Writers' Union to cover my expenses for this trip.

Declaration by Ismail Kadare
(24 October 1990)

My decision to leave my country is the natural extension of everything I have defended in my works up to this point.

Yesterday I addressed a letter to President Ramiz Alia in which I described my reasons for that action. Until now, I have tried to contribute to the softening of the regime as much as possible in Albania. Through meetings and an exchange of letters with the President last spring, I clearly expressed the great necessity of a democratization of the country that must be swift, deep and complete. But the promises made were not kept, and my disillusionment, like that of the majority of the Albanian people, has been so much more grievous.

Since I had no other means of expressing my point clearly and fully, because there is no possibility of lawful opposition, I have chosen this path, which I have never wanted to pursue and which I do not advise for anyone.

The Albanian people—those who live within the country's borders and those who live in Kosovo—now find themselves in the most dangerous period of their history. In this tragic hour no one can afford to act irresponsibly, adventurously or abusively, or to make claims of superiority. It is everyone's duty to avoid bringing about a catastrophe that would be irreparable for the country. Those who consciously or unconsciously provoke or support dangerous extremes shall in future be held responsible before history for their complicity in that crime.

The Albanian legislators must immediately give up their absurd and archaic judgements concerning liberty and the rights of man, question the grounds for repression of those rights, and above all their criteria in regard to the legitimacy of the ruling power. These conceptions, while based upon theory or pseudo-theory, are contrary to universal law and have already been banished in the civilized world. The Albanian legislators must understand that it is not democratization but its opposite that will lead it to its own undoing. They must seize the very last chance they have to save the country.

In this difficult phase the Albanians need more than ever to show cool-headedness, intelligence and spiritual high-mindedness. They must understand that in one way or another the responsibility for any epoch falls upon everyone, just as breaking with evil shall be the contribution and the merit of each person.

I should like to add that the family of European peoples should be a little more attentive to that nation whom history has treated with great severity. By helping that country escape the fate which has weighed her down for so long, and in making her an integral part of itself, Europe can make up for its past indifference.

One word more. I hope to return quite soon to my country. When I say that, I am not thinking of returning the day after catastrophe, but after the beginning of true democratization, which in my view is certain to come.

Ismail Kadare
24 October 1990

PART THREE

Hope

At a time when dictatorships, while rather like ancient tyrannosaurs marching to extinction, are nevertheless still with us, there is no doubt that we must talk about them. But it is ten times more urgent that we proceed with the autopsy, or give them an X-ray examination, with one special purpose: to be rid of them.

Imagine a cinema or a concert hall plunged into darkness, with its feebly lit 'EXIT' signs barely visible. In case of fire, a terrified crowd would surge through those doors. In a totalitarian country, when the first creakings can be heard, people's immediate reflex is to look for the safety exits. But unlike the cinema or concert hall, the safety exits of a dictatorship have signs with incomprehensible, not to say mysterious, inscriptions. For that reason, many people risk plunging into the abyss because they are headed for the wrong door.

People fall under the yoke of dictatorship in various ways, but everyone ends up in more or less the same condition—mutilated. One might fall under dictatorship suddenly, the result of a *coup d'état*, a foreign invasion, a revolution, a civil war, a counterrevolution. But one can also fall into it little by little, without noticing, over a long period of degeneration. And there is a third, almost paradoxical, way: one might enter dictatorship as one would go to a fair, or a party. In this case, too, if one goes to a dictatorship as one goes to a dance, one escapes it as if from an earthquake.

When Albania (one of the few countries in the world whose constitution stipulates that it live 'under the regime of the dictatorship of the proletariat') entered into a dictatorship of its own free will in November 1944, that entrance was really a sort of holiday.

Not only did a joyous atmosphere prevail everywhere: posters announced dances, sometimes even in French—*soirées dansantes*—concerts, parades and fashion shows, young people became engaged, and free love was practised more openly than ever before in that severe Balkan country. Everything was permissible. The press was free to say what it liked; along with the news of the outside world, one might read local news like this: 'Last night, the religious sect of the Bektashis performed a ceremony, with *roufai,*[*] in the presence of the Head of State, Mr Enver Hoxha.' Or announcements concerning Catholic worship in the great cathedral at Shkodra, or news of the capital city by the writer, Petro Marko. A pluralist vocabulary—words used 'without distinction of provinces, religions, or opinions'—could be heard everywhere. Authors with divergent viewpoints had been named to preside over the Writers' Union; the poet Lasgush Poradeci challenged a member of the communist government because of an insult.

The reverse of the medal were incidents that arose from the fact that everything was topsy-turvy. A growing violence was taking root; there were expropriations, lawsuits, arrests and executions— but it was all hidden by the tra-la-la of merrymaking. It's understandable, since the celebration of the Albanian communists was in tune with a worldwide celebration—fascism had just sunk into the abyss. The Albanian communists were on the side of the victors. They were enemies of the vanquished. The Albanian communists had been allied with the USSR, the United States, Britain. Inscriptions reading 'Roosevelt–Stalin–Churchill', together with their portraits, were seen everywhere, and it seemed quite natural that communist Albania decreed a day of mourning when President Roosevelt died.

At that time, nobody dreamed of criticizing the victors. They were the fortunate ones. One might say they'd been born with a caul, since they'd chosen the right side. And their good luck was redoubled because of the immediate sympathy they aroused: most partisans were young and dapper, and many among them were high-school

---

[*] Rituals in which dervishes dance, go into trances, etc.

boys. There were also professors and university students who, interrupting their studies in Rome, Vienna or Paris, had come home to fight; sons of the idealistic bourgeoisie who, fascinated by communist theories, had renounced their parents and their wealth; later, priests and other religious people from various confessions joined with them. Young women were another important element in the wave of popular sympathy. For the first time in Albanian history, thousands of girls, most of them under twenty, had taken part in the struggle. Opponents of the communists thought they had found the weak point at which to strike; putting stock in Albanian puritanism, they concentrated their abundant zeal in campaigns against the communists in the area of morality. Their argument was simple: the participation of the young girls in the movement proved that the communists had not gone into the maquis to liberate the country from fascism, as they claimed, but to have fun and to shirk real fighting.[1] Hadn't people always said that communism would destroy the family, and that all the women would be held in common by the men? In a country that acted as the moral citadel of the family, adhering rigorously to custom, here was something that sounded like the apocalypse. Besides, it was a country with a cult of masculinity, of the famous *Kanun** in which the epic gesture is part of the monopoly of Albanian men. Therefore, O ye brave, let us extirpate the bad communist seed before it overturns the foundations of the nation!

Nevertheless, to everyone's astonishment, the rigid Albanian nation showed unprecedented tolerance towards its young women. The country whose hand had never trembled at savagely punishing female disobedience actually took up the challenge. Instead of exploding in outrage, the people did just the opposite; it all seemed to please them. This was really something unheard of, and it gave the communists even more credibility when they declared that they were not only fighting to free the country but also to build a new world. In this way, favoured always by good fortune, the communists, far from

---

* The written depository of Albania's traditional oral laws and norms.

having to suffer from a duel with the moralists, emerged stronger than ever and gained still more sympathy. Knights-errant of freedom, they were the champions of liberalism, of a more beautiful life, and of a good deal more love.

Throughout the memorable autumn of 1944 and the winter of 1945, young women partisans, together with thousands of others, crowded the streets, having a good time, becoming engaged to boys they had known in the maquis, or to others whom they had just met, happy as you please. At the Hotel Dajti, where the upper middle class amused themselves, the day would dawn while the knights-errant were still dancing . . .

There is no way to explain what happened in Albania thereafter, nor what is happening today, without reference to this beginning. Most of the characters in the drama were twenty years old then; now they all are sixty-something. The whole of their lives—happiness, love, children—is rooted in that beginning. Whether they rose to high positions or remained unknown, or even if they were sent to prison, they still remain tied to that period with an incurable sense of nostalgia. For many of them the clock stopped then.

So the party was at its height in that winter of 1945, and no one knew what was hatching behind the scenes: intrigues, ongoing power struggles, the poison and the knife the leaders were preparing for one person or another. No one yet understood what 'the class struggle' meant, what was behind Stalin's smile, what messages the Yugoslav and Russian envoys carried, or who landed at night, semi-clandestinely, by torchlight, at Tirana airport. People understood even less why the Party, always present in speech, could never be found on the ground. No one knew who its members were, let alone its officials; as in Kafka's novels, no one even knew where its offices were, since they were hidden under various names: Front, Public Welfare, Youth Movement.[2] But even if people had known about all that, they still were ignorant of the most significant thing to come: Yalta. Whatever plans the nation might have had, whatever aspirations the people might have shared, the fate of Albania was sealed at Yalta. The new gods, like the Olympians but more pitiless, condemned Albania by setting her on the descending side of the balancing scale, that of the East.

Albania's last chance was taken up by Greece.

What might have happened had there been no meeting at Yalta? It's hard to say. But there is no doubt that things would have turned out differently. It's possible that Albania, while remaining communist —a path she herself had chosen from the start—might have become the first country in the world to develop a different form of communism. She should have been the first to tear herself away from the Red Empire. But that opportunity also fell to another: this time to Yugoslavia.

Albania's eventual break with the socialist camp, her troubles with the USSR and later with China, were only the last feeble expressions of an aspiration, one that should have manifested itself much earlier. Like a woman who has missed her best child-bearing years, and then suffers miscarriage after miscarriage, Albania paid dearly for that historic blunder.

Meanwhile, at Tirana airport, semi-clandestine emissaries carried mysterious messages. *Savoir faire* in the construction of detention camps, the surveillance of whole populations, the stifling of parliamentary opposition, the recruitment of spies. Others were experts in intensifying the class struggle, or developing new methods of torture, etc. It was surely on one of those nights that the foul plot was launched to place underwater mines in the Corfu Channel. The result was several damaged ships, and some dozens of British sailors killed. The Corfu incident, a wound that, half a century later, has still not healed, and that brought about the severing of diplomatic relations between Britain and Albania, marks the beginning of Albania's estrangement from Europe. From that incident to the time a barber was charged with cutting the long hair of foreigners at Tirana airport, there has been a long series of tragic, and sometimes comic, actions which have ensured the isolation Albania was seeking. The desire for isolation is one of the most painful chapters, and one of the blackest stains on the history of the Albanian people.[3]

What began with Britain following the explosion of a lurking mine, has been perpetuated by the terms of an unwavering policy that persisted for more than forty years. The linchpin of that policy was to elude, under any and all circumstances, contact with the Western world. Albania was to separate itself until the end of time. For eternity. Given that point of view, all means, occasions and pretexts were fair play. With Britain they used mines; with the Federal Republic of Germany it was war reparations; with the United States, they raised questions of high principle (imperialism, the enemy of the people, etc). Having succeeded in breaking relations with those three countries, Albania kept up a façade of goodwill with France and Italy. Nevertheless, its goodwill was quite cool. On the other hand, Albania proclaimed strong and cordial ties with a number of countries like Algeria, Tunisia, Turkey, etc, countries that for the most part had been governed by the Ottoman Empire—the nightmare Albania had just managed to throw off. The peoples of those countries proclaimed themselves 'fraternal Arab peoples', deeply shocking the Albanians, who, not content with racism (a trait that is decidedly not to their credit), saw in them a painful reminder of Islamic Turkish hegemony.

As if that were not enough, after removing Albania from the socialist camp, Enver Hoxha decided to build another rampart that would separate his country from Europe. In 1967 he banned religion and proclaimed Albania the most atheistic country in the world. That measure had no justification whatsoever, for in 1967, as in an earlier century, Albania's three religions caused no major problem. No, the motive was quite different—to create a new wall to separate Albania and Europe. A rampart can be a good deal more solid than a political cleavage. (It was not by chance that Catholicism, the most 'Western' of the three religions, was dealt the hardest blows.)

Hoxha's foresight could not have been more accurate. Once religion was prohibited, contempt for Albania grew stronger. But that's exactly what Enver Hoxha wanted—for the rest of the world to pay no attention to Albania, to forget her very existence.

That became even more patent in 1979 when, at the height of the worldwide execration of Stalin, Hoxha published his book *With*

Stalin, a shameless slap in the face of civilization. Many thought the book simply mad, but it was nothing of the kind. On the contrary, it was deliberate and premeditated. Scorn for and exasperation with Albania grew everywhere. Many people said, 'To hell with that country, I don't want to hear about it any more.' But no one tried to explain that the Head of State had been longing for just that outcome. 'Let them leave us alone.' To crown that abominable feat and kill hope once and for all, he announced this monstrous shibboleth: 'If your enemy insults you it means you are doing the right thing.'

Always the same arguments, always the same zeal in widening the rift between this country and the rest of the world, when the Constitution was amended with articles forbidding economic relations with other countries, or the underwriting of foreign credit, or the creation of joint enterprises with foreigners. If any one of these articles was breached, the penal code prescribed death.

To return to that grotesque personage, the barber of Rinas airport, he was no mere product of delirium. Foreigners by the dozen made a quick retreat, and the pair of scissors brandished by that psychopath was clearly the symbol of Enver Hoxha's dream: to cut off all relations with the rest of the world, now and for ever.

In those early years, 1944 and 1945, none of that could possibly have been predicted. Quite the contrary, in fact—until the day the mines exploded in the Corfu Channel.

The cold war had begun. After the departure of the British, the American embassy closed its doors; after the Americans left, Yugoslavs and Russians disembarked in Tirana and went about the city: What a blessing that the Westerners have gone. Now we're alone, no one is looking. Strike without pity, without let-up!

The jailing of deputies from the 'opposition group' followed by their trials and execution; the acts of violence against the clergy (particularly against Albanian Catholics, abhorred by the local communists and even more by Serbian communists); the settling of accounts not only with declared adversaries but with potential adversaries as well; arrests and sentences with or without trial—it all became commonplace.

The resignation of the Minister of Justice, M. Konomi, to protest at official violations of legality, marked the swift ending of an epoch.[4] Afterwards, the 'intensification of the class struggle' (a Marxist-Leninist euphemism for terror) became authorized carnage.

Once more, though fate was not smiling on Albania, the 'Lady of Misfortune,'* luck was still with the Albanian communists. In 1948, following the Titoist heresy, Albania and Yugoslavia became embroiled in conflict. Some people claimed (and rightly so) that the number-two man in the Albanian government, Koçi Xoxe, Secretary of the Central Committee of the Party and Minister of the Interior (in other words, the butcher and hangman of the country), was Yugoslavia's man. There was nothing easier than to blame him for everything that had brought about suffering, and it was easier still because his crimes were not few.

An appropriate trash bin for the offal of history. A Minister of the Interior of Slavic origin, sworn enemy of the intelligentsia, cruelty incarnate, ugly, short, unpolished, as compared with the handsome, distinguished, tall Enver Hoxha; crass ignorance compared to French cultivation—Koçi Xoxe provided a providential contrast.

People sighed with relief. The hallucination was coming to an end, and not a moment too soon. Now we can understand the nightmare. Now we can understand the indifference over Kosovo. At last, they've rectified this evil paradox, this friendship with the South Slavs that looked like a sin against nature, given the millennial hostility between the two nations—and worse, the loss (or more accurately, the sacrifice) of Kosovo.

The easing of tensions was palpable. Even afterwards, when it was clear that neither 'the class struggle' nor 'revolutionary violence' would be relaxed, and even when people no longer talked about Kosovo, they imagined nonetheless that civilization had chalked up a victory in Albania. To this day, forty years later, the people—rarely mistaken when they pin a label on one or another era—have baptized that dark time 'the time of Koçi'. In their daily struggle with the

---

* Poets of the nineteenth century referred to Albania by this name.

forces of darkness, the forces of democracy have often used the expression *Koçixoxism*, like a vaccine extracted from a poison.[5]

A violent campaign was mounted in Albania against Yugoslavia. However, even while Tito was being attacked, no one, anywhere, mentioned Kosovo, where half the Albanian nation suffered atrocious oppression. Tito was attacked solely for having violated the principles of Marxism-Leninism. Once again the communists demonstrated that for them doctrine was more important than anything else.

Some thought at the time that the sin of fraternizing with the South Slavs, the trouble in Kosovo, etc, could not be seriously altered because of the friendly ties with the Great Slavs, the Russians. But after 1960, when the break with the USSR was consummated, when, in the thousands of pages written by Enver Hoxha about China, there were barely more than a few lines about Kosovo, there was general despair in Albania.

However, 1960 was another lucky year for the Albanian communists. Quite independently of circumstances, the divorce with the Soviet camp (something the people had long dreamed about) seemed simply miraculous. New hopes, new disillusionments, new forms of trickery in the air. It was just the atmosphere that the totalitarian state required, particularly during a period of crisis when it was short of breath.

Other things also came along to bolster the good luck of the Albanian communists, even if only in a limited way. The vanquished class, particularly landowners and businessmen, hadn't left behind the slightest pleasant memory in the country. They hadn't even, at a minimum, erected handsome buildings that might have earned them a measure of admiration. As for King Zog, while he had been a soft, inoffensive tyrant, no one felt any nostalgia for his reign in Albania. Moreover, the two giants of Albanian letters, Fan Noli and Lasgush Poradeci, the first living in the United States, the other in Tirana, wrote nothing against the communist government in that period.[6]

Whether we get into a dictatorship through the gates of mourning or the gates of celebration, we discover that it is the same everywhere. It remains a poorly explored planet, even for those of us who have written a good deal about it, reflected long and hard about it and, further still, sunk into deep consternation over it. We speculate on the average life expectancy of dictatorship just as we might speak of the life expectancy of man, or dog, or crow. We elaborate on its various phases—its growth, its maturity, its old age and, no doubt, its death (ah!). Countless opinions have been expressed and treatises written, usually tiresome drivel, on the general level of the discussions at the local tavern to which we mortals are prone. These discussions are like conversations about the weather: it's getting cold, it's warming up, it will be another hard winter, I expect there will be wind, sun . . . The universal and commonplace engagement is understandable because dictatorship weighs upon each of us, or more precisely, it concerns the whole world. In all that jumble it is rare, most rare, that we draw any valuable lesson from it. In the last analysis, we have nothing more than that monotonous litany that portrays dictatorship. Even as it is vast and monotonous as the grains of sand in the Sahara, we are compelled to draw, for lack of anything better, upon isolated voices—one here, one there—in order to find, despite everything, some bit of evidence.

The claim has been made that dictatorship is at its best (plump and tasty, as one says of a fat hen at market) after about twelve years; it's also been suggested that it's heartiest at double that age. In any case, most people think that dictatorial regimes, even those built by a master hand and protected all round by anti-seismic barriers, do not last much more than forty years.

In symbolizing dictatorship, it has been shown that people sometimes refer to creatures, usually distasteful ones—dinosaurs, tyrannosaurs or many-headed hydras—and at other times to buildings: fortresses, pyramids, bunkers. This ambivalence, this plasticity, is nothing more than one of the numerous manifestations of the monstrous character of the phenomenon. Just as in the popular imagination the forces of hell draw power from an ability to change form in an instant, so dictatorship can only be seen for what it is, that is, multiform, two-faced, hybrid. Yet, unlike mythic creatures (witches or dragons) that take their diversity from within a single kingdom, dictatorship goes farther. As we've just seen, dictatorship can be associated with animals, with buildings; in other words, in our imagination it can be at the same time a thing with claws and with gates, it can be tiger and pyramid, dungeon and dragon. (If someone were to come and say that all this is only the fruit of our imagination, we should answer that what goes on in our imagination is an intimate part of what makes up reality.)

Such, then, is dictatorship; unfortunately, it is highly changeable, and therefore dangerous. It's not only because of its origins that one fine day the fanfares and little flags join in the fair, to be accompanied the next day by barbed wire. It's a sign of its very essence: reversible. That's why the ambivalence of its image is rightly considered to be a feature of its foundations.

In its early days (let's say at puberty), dictatorship can be harsh and irritable; yet despite the violence and terror which mark this phase, it's later, when dictatorship has reached a more advanced age, when it has mellowed, when it has donned the mask and begun to disguise its crimes, that it becomes most formidable. Having spat out its first venom, the dictatorship begins to think of the future, of its perpetuity. In practice, this usually happens near the age of ten to twelve years. This is the stage at which it begins to secrete its worst horrors, those things that it believes will be the prop of its old age. That fruitful period comes to an end around forty, the age at which it gives birth to its last monsters.

Since it is an organic mechanism, it engenders cells, separable parts: sensations, temperaments, laws, statutes, idols, sentimentality, intellectual intoxication, language, architecture, novels, music, morality, joy, despair—all of which become a new species: the offspring of dictatorship. It also becomes self-reproducing; it has no need, for example, to borrow from Roman or Asiatic law, because it can produce its own. And that goes for everything: no need for pity, for sex, for anything that makes a life . . .

One of Bulgakov's novellas, narrated in a banal tone as if what is being told is the most ordinary thing, the arrival of a character: 'At that time Vanya Diktaturovitch came and announced that   ', etc. In the context, the author's calm, his refusal to make any commentary from the beginning to the end of the story, is aimed at demonstrating in a most striking way how the dictatorship had by this time put down roots that were almost impossible to pull up. From the time it began sowing seeds in the language, the dictatorship succeeded, in part, in destroying that language. Now it is attacking proper nouns. It's approaching forty, the age at which it strives to become second nature; that is, to endow itself with a genetic code of its own making. From now on it is not just a matter of producing infrastructures, or walls and machines that carry its name. No, as Brodski has pointed out, it is straining to go even further—to ensure that its 'bricks' are new and original; that they are truly 'its own'. When that goal is reached, the dictatorship imagines it can escape all possible trouble in the future, particularly the burden of vigilant control of the security of its ramparts, and indeed of all its structures. Everything built with its own bricks, even though it may look like an imported object, will in fact be of the regime's own begetting.

We have been speaking of 'bricks', but clearly with something else in mind, 'the new man'. Naturally, the expression 'new bricks' is never mentioned in the regime's propaganda, yet millions of pages, hymns, songs, have been dedicated to the new man. That was one of the most stirring dreams of the dictatorship. And with good reason.

Achieving that goal, the breeding of a new man, would mean security for the regime's old age. The new man, *homo dictatorensis*, whatever he might do, whatever projects he might propose, his passion and the character of his work would always be marked by an instinctive loyalty to the dictatorship.

That was no chimera. Dictatorship in various countries had already achieved a measure of loyalty that was far from negligible. They had even succeeded in bringing forth both abusers and victims prone to turn against one another, but never against the regime. That explains why their internal quarrels, their battles and their crises often remain incomprehensible, even mysterious, to a candid eye and spirit. They look that way because, despite the fact that they're engaged in a fight to the death, their struggle always takes place far away, in a universe whose dimensions are very different. Each side, like the other, is a child of the dictatorship.

After its first successful attempts, the dictatorship tries to make its dream come true. It's the eve of its fortieth year, the hour of its last campaign. The third generation will soon arrive on the scene, under the dictatorship. It's the fulfilment of the human life cycle: child, parent, grandparent. That is the critical phase. The horizon grows more and more uniform. A disheartening grey spreads everywhere, just as it had in those mythical times when Prometheus ascended to Zeus, telling him of his anger over the fact that mankind was becoming weakened, washed out, degenerate . . .

The dictatorship tries to succeed where the Greek Zeus failed completely. And it's at this critical moment that dictatorship lets out the first sounds of cracking.

The first signs of cracking generally come when the tyrant dies. The time that elapses between that moment and the overthrow of the dictatorship varies enormously from country to country. In the Soviet Union, dictatorship and the period of de-dictatorialization (1917–1953–1986) lasted just about the same time, about thirty-five years. In Romania the first cracks following the death of the tyrant and the dissolution of the regime took place within two or three days, but it is difficult to estimate how much time must elapse before the dictatorship is actually overthrown—an event which should not be confounded with its fall. In Albania, it would seem that the uprooting of the dictatorship will take several years, but certainly not as long as in the Soviet Union. As for other countries of Eastern Europe, estimates of the actual number of years are hard to arrive at because, although the duration of dictatorship proper is well known (1945–1953), opinions vary about the length of the other phases: post-Stalin dictatorship, flexible dictatorship, post-dictatorship.

The case of Romania must be considered separately, due to a factor peculiar to that country. After the phase of dictatorship proper, the phase shared by all East European countries, and after the relative liberalization of Khrushchev, Romania fell under a second dictatorship, this time even more absurd because it was imposed by a common *apparatchik*, a person totally lacking in charisma. Without doubt, that peculiar fact explains why twice-dictatorial Romania was the only nation to execute its tyrant as it would have executed a common criminal.

The case of Romania reminds the world that there is another manner of breaking away from communist dictatorship: through violent death, massacre, terror. That kind of rupture appeals to some as epic-heroic, Shakespearian, more spectacular than bidding farewell to communism as in Czechoslovakia or Hungary, for example. Epithets aside, it's safe to say that whatever the verdict of history, one thing is certain about the epilogue in Romania: it has the aftertaste of dictatorship. In other words, despite its romantic air, its epic cast, something gives the impression that those people who rushed forth heroically to destroy the tyrant, at the very instant when they held him by the throat, unknowingly fulfilled some secret clause in his will.

That may seem odd, but it is really not odd at all. Among numerous offspring of the dictatorship there is one most formidable: the epilogue, the scenario of its own death. That is, having given birth to people, language, states of mind, landscapes and poets—in short, a complete flora and fauna destined to people the dictator's desert—the dictator, in an effort to close the circle, brings into being a final offshoot, perhaps his favourite, the comfort of his old age: the very diagram of his own death. A death by subterfuge, through which the dictatorship hopes to renew itself.

We all know that death by violence is the kind of death that begets still more death and crime. The secret desire of dictatorship is for an epilogue of hatred and blood. A careful study of the chronicles of tyranny—of its press, its propaganda, its art and philosophy, its archives—confirms that the obsession with death is a dominant feature. Albania will die in her tracks, but she will not betray

Marxism-Leninism! Serbia may be destroyed, but she will never give up Kosovo! Romania will die for the doctrines of Ceauçescu! The island of Cuba will be drowned in the sea, but it will not renounce socialism! Iraq will explode, but it will not yield to the United States! . . .

Songs, novels, doctoral theses, autumn festivals—all are meant to remind us of death; and not infrequently, thousands of people give their consent to that premature obituary.

Meanwhile, the dictatorial state, having built tunnels and bunkers where its leaders can take shelter, having arranged, more or less in secret, airfields from which the last of them may flee abroad, has drawn up lists of people who are to be shot at the first sign of disorder. (If we are really defeated, you'd better make up your mind that you won't live to enjoy it. We'll shoot you first.)

These lists, though nominally secret, are circulated here and there with perfect cynicism, especially at meetings of government officials. ('Comrades, what we say here is strictly between us, all communists. I want to tell you, in strict confidence, that, whatever happens, the Party has taken measures so as not to be caught napping. We have drawn up lists . . .')

It goes without saying that this kind of terror by list makes the entire nation tremble.

It's no more and no less than the conduct of bandits under siege. Death becomes their universe, their philosophy, their only escape hatch; it inspirits them and plunges them into an ugly ecstasy. Dictatorship always smells of death, but in its last moments that odour becomes its natural aroma. It's used to it and can no longer shake it off.

In its last delirium, the dictatorship tries to fool the world by taking credit for the whole of the heroic tradition of humanity. It fixes its eyes on Prometheus, whose myth, disfigured by vulgar romanticism, by the ignorant and the terrorists, by mediocre writers and the inevitable exhibitionists, is now easy prey. Not only does Prometheus have absolutely nothing to do with dictatorship's brand of hero, but he is its very antithesis. He's much closer to the

Sakharovs of this world (even if the fire he has given mankind, the H-bomb, is, in accordance with ancient Greek thought, an 'exaggerated fire', and therefore evil). But if Prometheus resembles the Sakharov who was interned in Gorki (Sakharov chained), he resembles more Sakharov freed, and even more the Sakharov in the third play of the trilogy, when he takes his place on Olympus (the Kremlin) as a deputy.

Prometheus was never the hero of useless sacrifice; on the contrary, he is the hero of intelligence and reason. Indeed, it was through reason, not blind obstinacy, that Prometheus won his victory and saved humankind. And mutual concessions between Zeus and Prometheus, tolerance and dialogue, are the essence of his myth. It might be entitled *The Drama of Dialogue*. If the first part of Aeschylus' trilogy—the only one preserved to us—is about the impossibility of dialogue, the other two must mark its triumph.

More faithfully than any other, this myth testifies to the sufferings that humanity has borne—terror, chains, destruction—to reach Olympus (i.e. Parliament) and to send their first deputy to it. Since then, in the halls of Parliament, people have ceased to hear only a single voice, the voice of Zeus. From that viewpoint, to use a term from our own era, we might say that the myth of Prometheus emerges particularly as the triumph of pluralism. If mankind finds itself today at that level of emancipation, it's because long ago Prometheus had already reached that height.

Abandoning the obsession with death is a harbinger of flexibility in a dictatorship. For that very reason, perhaps we should help it then, in that time when its brain is numb and its eyes blind. The point for the manoeuvre is not to fall under its charm or into its pitfalls, but to avoid them intelligently. Then, when its last hour is come, seeing that it will die alone, and that in place of its vain epilogue the people have chosen a different path and a different banner, it will know dread and bitter torment. And then, in agony and dismay, it will tumble into hell.

Anyone who has lived under a dictatorship has imagined these last moments, even when it seemed there could be no hope, even at the century's darkest midnight. And when dawn approaches, we can imagine that people are not wholly preoccupied with locating the emergency exit. Everyone knows that the last hour has something fatal within it; for that reason they are assailed by their thoughts, which are most often painful. Solzhenitsyn compares that time to the moment when a building is about to crumble, and people below are wondering where to go so that they won't stop lumps of concrete with their heads. Others, whatever comparisons they may be thinking of, agree on one point: it's a dangerous moment.

Defying dictatorship under these circumstances is one common attitude; pursuing a dialogue with it is heroic. In defying the government one is faced with but a single adversary. However, in pursuing a dialogue with the regime, there are two things to fear: the government and the most impatient of its opponents. To help a dictatorship throw off even a small part of the evil it harbours is an enormous undertaking. If one does not succeed, all future attempts might be rendered impossible. The more so when the evil is deep-rooted, and one must work wonders to 'exorcise the demons of an entire nation.' However, if the forces of democracy succeed in ridding dictatorship of its obsession with death—just as the venom might be removed from a serpent or bombs taken from terrorists—then one can say that they have achieved their first important victory.

The obsession with death is tied to the idea of punishment, and therefore of being at fault. To free it completely from that obsession—which, even if renounced, could, in a moment of panic, be seized again temporarily—the totalitarian state, half-disoriented by the crisis, must still be helped. Helped to understand in what way and to what extent it is culpable, and what punishment it deserves.

This is a fundamental point for everyone, but especially for peoples like the Albanians for whom the right punishment (traditional vengeance) has long been one of the bases of their ancient Code and their moral concepts.

When one hears it said that responsibility for the injustice of the dictatorship must fall upon everyone, as Vaclav Havel so nobly declared a year ago, the first question that comes to mind must be: Is that really the case? Or is it merely a trick to fool the dictatorship (one of the many stratagems used by the police to get criminals to lay down their arms)?

Once the sincerity of the assertion is established (Havel, the writer, kept his word when he became president), other questions arise, some of them poisonous: How is that conceivable? How is it possible to share the blame? Why, it offends the memory of its victims and those who opposed tyranny! That's exactly what the regime wants to hear!

Sharing the blame is in fact a dream of the dictatorship—actually, it is much more than a dream. Throughout the period of its rule, the dictatorship, using any means possible, has done nothing but cast blame day and night. Making people guilty is something the totalitarian regime has come to bank on. The machinery for this purpose works in two different directions which seem totally unconnected. One of these is the remission of sins; the dictatorship inherited that from religion. The formula, 'All men are sinners in the eyes of God,' has been modified by substituting the word Party for the word God. Thus we are all guilty in Its eyes. The Party alone is infallible, we owe everything to Its grace, our daily bread, our life, our country. The words, '*Ave Partia gratia plena*' shouldn't seem out of place in a farce of this sort, since there are hundreds of songs and poems with even more outrageous praise, in which the word '*Ave*' is replaced by 'Glory' and the word 'merciful' by 'generous'!

At every step it is fitting to express one's gratitude to the Party. For every 'sin' there is a rite of confession before the Party. In 1975, because of my poem *The Red Pashas*, I was accused of having called for armed rebellion, which was simply not true. Nevertheless, I was forced to admit that 'unintentionally, I had launched an appeal for an armed uprising.' (I was permitted only to add the word 'unintentionally'.) I was required to put my confession in writing; the document must still be filed in the Party archives. It was an indictment set down in my own hand, which the government could use against me whenever it chose, and I knew it.

In the letter that Ramiz Alia addressed to me on 21 May 1990, he had written specifically: 'You must not forget what Enver Hoxha did for you.'

For decades my ears were accustomed to remarks of that kind, made as often by dignitaries of the Albanian regime as by people who were simply naive: He's protected by Enver Hoxha; He ought to show some gratitude to Enver Hoxha . . . In saying such things, they rarely asked themselves: From whom is Enver Hoxha protecting that writer? Isn't he protecting him from his own government? From himself? For everyone knew that the people attacking me were his faithful servitors, close colleagues or members of the Sigurimi.

In mentioning Enver Hoxha's protection of me as if it were an oddity, an anomaly, an exception to the rule, the Albanian bureaucracy gave the show away. According to communist logic, Enver Hoxha should not have allowed that writer to live. By ignoring the law, by abandoning principle(!), he had made a concession. And, accordingly, that writer should have been grateful. In short, I should be grateful to Enver Hoxha for protecting me from Enver Hoxha. (In my book *Invitation to the Writer's Studio*, in the only chapter I could not print in Albania, I explain in detail the mystery of that 'protection', which directly concerned my novel *The Great Winter*, the book that was my life jacket and at the same time my curse. I myself could have been killed, but that book, that book had to survive. Yet for it to live I would have to die 'with honour'. That is, I would have to die one of those deaths that end in a funeral covered with flowers and praise.[7])

As the dictatorship prospers, feelings of guilt begin to predominate. But in expanding, the guilt also becomes soft and blurred, until the moment arrives when the fog is everywhere: people feel guilty without knowing what they are guilty of.

That constitutes one of the triumphal phases of dictatorship: the time when guilt, fear, and submissiveness come together in a nameless vapour. ('What are we compared to the Party? Zero!'—it was with these words that an ambassador opened a morning conference at the Albanian embassy in Vienna. 'We need not blush if we are accused of servility to the Party,' another person declared at a meeting of the Writers' Union.)

Another aspect of shared guilt is even more vital to tyranny because it concerns its very existence, or more precisely, the day on which it will be judged. Every dictatorship, no matter how much it blusters and swaggers about its invincible power, has serious forebodings. For that reason, even though it forces itself not to think of its coming end, it is always preparing for it. And to place blame—for its own actions, this time—on the largest number of people, if possible on the whole body of its citizens, is one of its primary objectives.

The connection with crime, and therefore with guilt, spun in the prophetic manner of Dostoevsky in his novel *The Possessed*—when the crime, committed together, of killing their fifth comrade 'strengthens' the group of four revolutionaries—is the way in which the dictatorship has drawn up its basic programme. It is not upon four people but four thousand, four hundred thousand, four million if possible, that it must try to lay the blame. The regime reasons that in this way, when hard times come, it will not only save itself from attack but will be protected by collective guilt.

The dream of the totalitarian state, then, is to make guilt universal. But before reaching that point, the dictatorship will have tried to rid itself of responsibility by other means. One method in vogue is a reliance on 'Vice-' so and so, a title that often masks the identity of the real leaders. (From the Vice-Commissioners of the anti-fascist struggle in Albania to Vice-President Deng Xiaoping, the leader of China, there is a long list of masked persons who have pulled the strings behind the curtain so as not to be exposed to either danger or hatred.) The idea no doubt came from the Islamic world where the Caliph, though called the Lieutenant of God, was in reality lord and master.

For modern dictatorships, however, this strategy has had its limitations; that is why, one after another, they have turned to the wholesale sharing of blame.

The sharing of blame is carried from one circle to the next. In the beginning, the dictator and his family dispense blame in the zone nearest them, which can be called the first zone, the one including other members of the government. These people are drawn into the circle of guilt through the artifice of decisions, plenary sessions, decrees and the classic bestowal of privileges. The second zone might be the circle of close colleagues—judges, prosecutors, and particularly members of the Sigurimi, 'the beloved arm of the Party'. In the third zone (as we see, this is all taking on considerable mass), we find the most fanatic militants, the army of Party secretaries, the border guards (the killers), etc. The fourth circle, particularly vast and dark, is that of spies and informers. Some have joined the ranks out of conviction, and others because they were in serious trouble; together they make up the group which the regime can most safely rely on. Though they were entrapped for very different reasons—through some unhappy personal circumstance, to serve a trivial need, as the result of a swindle or some shameful act, for men homosexuality, for women adultery,[8] etc—each of them is registered by name in secret files, and while they may hate the dictatorship like everyone else, they are afraid to see it overthrown. The fifth circle is that of the intelligentsia: scholars, writers, artists, academicians. Quite apart from any personal zeal, and as a result of varying circumstances, they've become encrusted in that world to which, like it or not, they are attached. Some of them joined out of genuine enthusiasm, because that world was made to measure for them; most of them however, the most talented, have suffered from it. Caught in the tragic dilemma between giving up creativity in order not to serve the regime, and in that case to be of no use to their countrymen who have so great a need for their creativity—between that path, therefore, and the other path, which is to fight for enlightenment even under the dictatorship, many choose the latter. This latter choice is immediately regarded as complicity, not only by the regime but by a crowd of spectators, particularly foreign spectators, who feel no compassion and don't trouble themselves about the needs that the country in question may or may not have regarding culture and enlightenment. The dictatorship, however, shrewder than a con artist, is the first to suspect the co-culpability of the creative element. Accordingly, it never stops hammering away at the guilt of the intelligentsia, using for that purpose declarations and testimonials extorted by violence (adding, for example, the word 'Party' to a scientific article written by the great linguist Eqrem Çabej); and if testimonials are not forthcoming, the regime manages to make them up out of whole cloth.[9] The sixth circle includes those who are being indoctrinated, especially the schoolchildren. It's the most unstable zone because it is like a transit camp—the generations are simply passing through. For all that, the regime doesn't hesitate to exploit that reserve army as often as necessary in order to stir up movements and disturbances. The seventh and final zone is more ample still: it is the zone of amorphous crowds, those who fill the stadiums when there are parades, and the public squares with noise and song when there are mass meetings. These public assemblies, even if we take into account that they are semi-obligatory, serve the dictatorship in two ways: first, they discourage potential opposition by reinforcing the 'unity of the people'; second, they bolster the courage of the regime and its partisans. One special zone, occupied by 'foreign friends', paid charlatans, naive people, psychopaths and perverts, can be excluded from this classification in the same way that pagans are excluded in Dante's Hell.

In this way, the dictatorship has spread the responsibility for its crimes everywhere, or believes it has. If one takes as a model the derivation of the word 'musician' from the word 'music', we might just as well call the dictatorship by the name CRIMINAL. And the regime feels authorized to say to everyone: We have acted together in everything, hence, if we must die, we shall all die together.

The fate of many lives depends on the last dialogue with dictatorship. One could say, 'Sorcerer, you will die alone, while we go on living!' That will not stop the coming of tragedy, but, on the contrary, will precipitate it. One might also say, 'That's enough of the word *death*. We have a banner, the banner of life.' Now, that would be much more reasonable. But to reach that point, the people—those who, without realizing it, hold in their hands the keys of history, thanks to the numberless possibilities that are theirs and theirs only—must make the regime understand that dictatorship's own epilogue, violent overthrow, is not inevitable. And neither will its overthrow bring about the surest death of a dictatorship. Its definitive death will come only when we have cut off its roots and turned aside the springs that feed it. Indeed, the word 'overthrow' must be replaced with the words 'drying up.' A dried-up dictatorship is more dead than a dictatorship overthrown.

Finding the roots and springs that nourish a totalitarian system is not simple. Some can be seen easily, others cannot. That the universe of guilt neighbours, indeed merges with, the universe of fear is clarity itself. That that kind of fear does not resemble the fears of earlier times is also obvious. It is fear of a new sort, quite specific, so that rather than speaking of a 'new man', more or less mythical, the communist world can be proud to have given birth to a 'new anguish', a 'new distress', the true product of its own making.

That sort of fear is peculiar to itself, since it does not merely have to do with the police, the army, prisons, tribunals and brutality, but with a broader arrangement of elements. Like the mechanics of guilt, it has its mysterious side, with ill-defined borders, as if in a dense mist. It shows up under different masks that at times look like adoration, enthusiasm, joy, ecstasy and masochistic pleasure, and at times like a grimace of horror. Those who wear these masks do not understand what they have in the depths of their hearts. They may hate the tyrant, but in his presence, at a meeting or in a conference hall, that hatred vanishes for no apparent reason. They may grumble at him every day, but when his car pulls up in the factory yard, their faces smile all by themselves, they forget their rancour against him, it seems natural to them to applaud.

What that means is that something has happened inside them a long time ago. A certain equilibrium has been disturbed. Other relations have been created, abnormal ones. In that change, fear (a horrifying fear, permanent, untiring) has played a primordial role.

Fear of that sort cannot take root in a normal life. The first thing the dictatorship does before instilling that fear is to attack normal life. There is the breaking down of perspectives, of points of view, of traditional relations—all of which are replaced by new perspectives, new visions, new relations.

The task is both simple and complex. Let us try to imagine how a campaign of fear is put into motion. (One of those campaigns that, now and then, come along to bruise the world black and blue.) The scenario goes more or less as follows.

The first phase, before the storm: there are murmurs here and there that something has happened. Someone has discovered something bad. So, something bad is going to happen. That is quite enough to impel people to make their first split with ordinary life. So and so was dreaming of a marvellous plan. Someone else was looking forward to his winter vacation. A third person was busy fixing up an apartment that he finally got after several years of waiting. Another man was wholly taken up with a woman he had just met, with the book he was writing, with the next football game. The very first rumours stop all of them in their tracks. Wait a moment, something is going to happen. In everything the rhythm falters, a void spreads everywhere. The memory of earlier campaigns, which seemed to be forgotten, comes back suddenly. The ear catches new sounds that it hasn't heard before. The eye sees shadows. All the senses are sharpened, are on the watch, and that is why the effect is multiplied many times when the gong of calamity booms.

The calamity explodes. You are frightened, of course, though you also feel a certain relief.

But the feeling of relief lasts a short time, because the machine is designed to work in phases, one after the other. After the first arrests comes a new period of anxious waiting: the period of investigations. A golden period for the regime, called 'uncovering the roots'. Hundreds of people ask themselves in terror if their name won't show up somewhere in the file.

But the regime is not content with these meagre reactions. At the very moment when you are no longer in a state of suspense, it proceeds to a new level of escalation. From vertical digging (uncovering the roots), it goes on without giving notice to make a horizontal leap. That is, it extends its attack to other circles that thought themselves to be out of danger. The years 1972 and 1973 are typical.

The blow fell in the area of culture. The bourgeois-revisionist influence on culture. Deviations in literature and in art. The discovery of the group of T. Lubonja and F. Paçrami. At that time, the period in which the whole creative intelligentsia was under pressure, official circles—particularly military men—not only imagined they were outside the line of fire, but felt they had the right to philosophize, too: So, you writers, you incorrigible liberals, we warned you that this would happen!

Well, the disaster that overtook them suddenly was even more terrifying. There was a putschist group. There were death sentences, starting with the Minister of War. There were executions.

Government technocrats had scarcely any time to amuse themselves at the expense of writers and the military (caprice, laurels, promotion) because misfortune came down upon them without warning. A hostile group in the nation's economy. Acts of sabotage in oil production. (During that decade, the Albanian petroleum industry produced more plots and sub-plots than it did motor fuel and other products.)

After culture, the army and the economy were stricken. Everyone understood that from then on anyone was vulnerable and anyone might be the next to suffer. A state of general paralysis had begun.

The attack on groups is among the favoured techniques of the dictatorship. That gives us a view of Marxist-Leninist science and procedure in explaining the world (culture, army and economics are classed as superstructures; dictatorship of the proletariat as structure—all of which are in the sights of the international bourgeoisie, while we have been teaching the classics of Marxism!). But if the tactic of focusing on groups is a favourite, that happens because they combine splendidly with the general sense of guilt and generalized fear.

It is fed by other factors as well. Among these, the mystery attack, the attack for no reason, is of particular interest. The attack for no reason reverberates after conviction, even after the victim is dead and buried.

Then there is the shot in the dark, among the most terrible weapons of the dictatorship. It confers on the government an ideal dimension, that of *fatum* (destiny). No one can imagine himself in the clear; the shot in the dark can fell anyone.

The shot in the dark, the attack for no reason, and the paradoxical attack are so many cogwheels in the mechanism of fear. The paradoxical attack includes inexplicable sentences pronounced against faithful servants of the regime. No one knows on what grounds these are based, but given the fact that these persons were hated by the people, the sentences meted out arouse a kind of general satisfaction. But the essence of it is that, over and above giving satisfaction, it supports the belief in the impartiality of justice. (In the course of one plenary session, Enver Hoxha addressed one of the most fanatical members of the Central Committee, D. Mamaqi, in these terms: 'In the last plenary session, I noticed that you, Comrade Mamaqi, behaved like a particularly remarkable hysteric, and that you were noisily rejoicing when we passed sentence on Todi Lubonja and A. Mero. Now let's discuss your own transgressions!')[10]

Those words could not fail to arouse a certain kind of sympathy among a number of people ('Enver Hoxha is a hard man, but a fair one! He can't stand cowards!') and to give some meagre consolation to those who had been attacked.

Generally speaking, the sentencing of high-ranking officials was a phenomenon of the palmy, victorious times of the regime; the effect of those measures was produced by the deep fog that surrounded them, but also because they seemed to be a contradiction in terms. On the one hand, they sowed panic everywhere, confirming the all-powerful aspect of the government; on the other, terror could not but be followed by a sickly satisfaction. (They're devouring one another. Good for them! In this world you pay for everything in the end. Their privileges will be their misfortune.)

When the condemned officials had been particularly brutal, the public satisfaction was all the greater, which the regime took as a sign of the people's support for the Party.

If, on the contrary, they met with public sympathy, as in the case of Todi Lubonja and A. Mero, the government turned a deaf ear. But given the fact that most of the condemned officials were detested, the government won most of the time. In this complex lottery, Enver Hoxha, who was remarkably artful, went to great lengths to manage that kind of business so that for every blow he struck there was always some group to find satisfaction in it. (The storm over the intellectuals, for example, made the Sigurimi rejoice; a blow aimed at the Sigurimi thereafter brought delight to the intellectuals.) But Enver Hoxha also aimed at gaining a premium in the case of notable people. When it came to Todi Lubonja and A. Mero, though Hoxha knew he could count on the support of the Sigurimi and of all the fanatics, he did not forget to offer a bit of consolation to the intellectuals by means of his belated retort to D. Mamaqi. He knew that his remarks wouldn't be noticed by the unenlightened fanatics (he did not mean to ruin their pleasure), but that they would be taken up at once by the intelligentsia who were in trouble at the time.

All these low manoeuvres, these mean hopes, make for a sort of numbness that develops into general anaesthesia. No flicker of opposition is registered anywhere. It is great good luck if one can remember that opposition is a matter of attitude. For the regime never lets you catch your breath. It gives you no respite. All you need is a quiet moment in which to pant. A little rest so you can recover. You are not in a condition that allows you to think—you're waiting for the storm to subside. You count the days, the hours. You don't feel hatred because that bitter taste has not had an instant in which to develop. Night and day you feel an emptiness in your stomach. A nameless emptiness, like a death pang, but worse. You hope for rest, but the government has taken measures so that there is no rest. Then, to make you despair absolutely, the government proclaims its intentions in its speeches: The enemy asks for a truce so that it can carry on with its plots, but the Party is vigilant! Stalin has taught us to give the enemy no time to breathe. So has Lenin and all the classics of Marxism.

The enemy, as it happens, is the entire people, who want to live. To live a normal life. That's all.

But a normal life is the worst enemy of the totalitarian state. It has done everything in its power, for the longest time, to disfigure that life, to tear it to tatters, substituting a caricature, an ersatz figure for human existence. The regime has disfigured it by organizing poverty, by rationing food, by making housing precarious, by imposing passports for domestic travel, by demanding voluntary work on Sunday, by holding endless meetings, by military training, by confiscating the peasant's cattle, by closing churches and cafés, by forbidding a free market, etc. It has achieved all that by rotating officials, a calamity that has scattered families to the four quarters of the country, and has destroyed so much human happiness. But it didn't stop there. Its vigilance has denounced dancing, denounced love. (How many people have been sentenced, have been severely punished? And by whom? By the same officials who, when they came down from the mountains in 1944, brandished among other banners the banner of love!) The government has been equally vigilant about the exchange of visits, and especially opposed to dinner invitations. The Secretary of the Tirana Party Committee has criticized those things several times. (Some year ago, another bigwig in Tirana, P. Miska, formerly a chauffeur and now a member of the Politburo, proposed severe economy measures (really for the purpose of ruining dinners); he had all electricity to the capital cut off, but was forced to give it up because leaflets opposing the government were being circulated everywhere while the city was in darkness.)

For someone who has not lived in that world, all of this might seem to be wholly imaginary. To present evidence of the truth of this scene, I need only mention the café business. People have not yet got over their rage on the subject. In the course of the summer of 1972, when it was known that President Nixon was going to China, Enver Hoxha, who was in the city of Durrës, called the entire Politburo into session. The people who were present at that assembly said they had felt that they were attending a wake. He sat there, scowling. Then, when he began to speak about what he thought would happen in China, he said in a failing voice, 'Now, over there, they are going to open the cafés again!'

During the winter of that year, the festival of song that was broadcast by radio and television, or more exactly, the pretty, long dresses of the announcers and the general atmosphere of gaiety in the hall, together with the elegance of the audience, provided a pretext for the storm directed against certain 'bourgeois revisionist influences in the culture'. That festival sounded the death knell for Todi Lubonja, at that time Director of Radio and Television. (Several years earlier, the holiday atmosphere in the hall of the National Theatre during the run of the play *Brown Stains* by M. Jero, the most charming play of the period, was the reason for banning the work and convicting the author.)

I remember having met Lubonja on the Grand Boulevard right after the first meeting of the Plenum of the Central Committee[11] in which the hurricane had begun to gather force. The session was deeply troubled, full of foreboding. Enver Hoxha had delivered a speech. When, among other things, he quoted those people who had testified about the influence of 'the bourgeois way of life' and had declared, 'Some comrades came to report that to me. I didn't believe them—yet they were right,' Kadri Hazbiu, the Minister of the Interior, applauded triumphantly, showing quite openly that he was the one who had delivered the denunciation. The things mentioned by Enver Hoxha on that subject included this remark: 'Young women are drinking cognac at the café.' (The cafés were places so abused thereafter that they were renamed confectioners, and the shop signs testified to the change.)

'Things are going badly for me,' Todi Lubonja said. When, to reassure him, I said that once more everything would work out as it had before, he answered, 'I don't think so. I'm afraid that heads will roll.'

After a brief silence, in his half-serious, half-joking way, he added, 'You told me that you were writing a novel about the beheading of high Turkish officials. Look and see if there isn't a little room for my head, too.'

'I have a spot for you,' I said in the same tone. 'I'm going to call you Todi Pasha, or better, since your name isn't appropriate for the Ottoman world, I'll give you a qualifying name, say, 'the Congenial Pasha'. (In that novel, *The Niche of Shame*, which I completed while he was in prison, he appears as 'the Blond Pasha'.)

A few weeks later, on a rainy afternoon, when he was within two inches of disgrace, Elena and I were visiting him, and Ramiz Alia's wife* came in. She was a good-hearted woman, and like many women who had taken part in the anti-fascist movement when they were young, she still had about her the candid idealism of that period. The atmosphere was bleak. She tried to kindle warmth and hope for the couple. She kissed Todi's wife, saying, 'Trust me, just another self-criticism and everything will be all right.' She said that with the stubbornness that people show in their repeated prayers to God. Those words came from the heart, and they were connected not only with Lubonja's fate but with her own—more particularly that of her husband, who, as Director of Propaganda, was at the time a target of the regime, and in serious trouble.

That was the last time I saw Todi Lubonja.

Sentences were meted out, one after the other. Culture, the army, the economy—whose turn would come next? The dictatorship made sure that nothing was left untouched, so that the anaesthesia would not be dissipated. Judicial debates are a feature of the stupefying and brutalizing of the people. And the servility of those who have been condemned helps to perpetuate the general paralysis. (B. Balluku, the Minister of Defence, goes to prison holding a picture of Enver Hoxha in his hand. Former generals, now condemned, take with them his complete works. One eery spectacle: P. Gusho, member of the Central Committee, who was accused of sabotage in oil production, commits suicide, and his relatives appear on the balcony, singing.)

Running parallel with this process, in the course of painful public

---

* She died in 1986.

meetings, the relatives of the condemned recite their self-criticisms, give details, confess and censure themselves. Other people not being threatened experience terrible inner changes amounting to mutilations of their characters. Conformism finds out the most devilish ways to confirm itself. For example, they know that the condemned are innocent, but none will say it. They are decent enough not to call the condemned people enemies of the state in private conversation, but the epidemic of guilt has so ravaged them that they do in fact find fault with the victims. ('It's true that 'X' was arrogant. The other charges I don't agree with, but he certainly was haughty and scornful.') They avoid dealing with the question in these terms: Can you condemn a man to fifteen years in prison for arrogance? Each in his own way salves his conscience, but his courage does not go beyond that. Like everything else in that world, courage is disfigured too.

The softening effect of conformism is such that they find it pleasant to believe that the condemned persons 'must have something to reproach themselves for, after all'. Or again, 'All of Enver Hoxha's anger cannot be entirely unfounded.' The mystery about the leader's rage is one of the techniques of confusion. It's accompanied by the most extreme caricature of the victims—for example, the Plenum called its former young favourite, Kadri Hazbiu, 'the marsh darky' since his complexion was swarthy and he liked duck-shooting; that helped make him a ready target.

The most astonishing thing is that the condemned could easily founder in those muddy depths themselves. As far as they were concerned, they knew they were not traitors; but when it came to other people, they couldn't help believing in their guilt.

Their conscience, and with it their intelligence, failed more and more, and each of them thought, 'How long, O Lord, will the terror last?'

Some said until March, some April. Others, more pessimistic, preferred not to name a date. Sorely tried, they wanted nothing but a respite. Truce in battle. At last the first signs of calm could be seen. A pale, cold sun rose on the horizon. Beneath the life that had been trodden down, the shoot, stiffened, began to sprout.

When we speak of the forces opposed to tyranny, we are likely to forget that those forces are not uniquely privileged in the struggle, and we forget what the real struggle is: the one in which the dictatorship and ordinary human life come to grips. A struggle more vast, more extended in time and tireless, by which the fate of both camps is settled.

The totalitarian state tries to create a 'new life', a 'new man'. But life resists, retreats slowly, attempts a counter-attack. Tiring itself in this battle, it also tires the dictatorship. The regime has police, the army, Party militants, newspapers, television, the classics of Marxism-Leninism. Life has an infinite army, unorganized, anonymous, in which the rank and file is something like this: young women who, despite their poverty, try to dress well and wear their hair in the current fashion; men and women who go to dine (to dine with others, as is done all over the rest of the world); people who speak a normal language, exempt from the monstrous Marxist coinage; invincible women who—defending themselves against all the pressures of the Party, the appeals to the class struggle and to vigilance against the enemy, etc—fall in love and make love; young men who get together for a drink, or simply to be bored in a human way; old people who make the sign of the cross; old women who feel pity; people who whisper, as in New York or in Zurich, Good Lord, how quickly winter came!'

This band that appears in no analytical report, no chronicle, no police file, this imaginary army—that is what will destroy the dictatorship. Because it is the deep well in which the modes of life are stockpiled. Unless it destroys those things, the dictatorship cannot destroy life. And unless it destroys normal life without replacing it with its 'new life', the dictatorship has no future. There is not room enough in the world for both of them. It's one or the other.

The fields in which the battle takes place are innumerable. To classify them, if we were to make the attempt, would be hopeless. Here are a few of them.

Apartments. As a staff general foresees the line of defence in a future war, the totalitarian state has taken preventive measures so that the buildings in which people live—the field in which one of the decisive battles will take place between mankind and itself—are planned to favour its triumph and the defeat of man. They must be sorry things, greyish, uncomfortable, and—this is important—as small as possible. As it happens, 'as small as possible' is the number-one priority of the dictatorship. That discourages man, impoverishes him spiritually, crushes him, exasperates him. In those bare, narrow cages that are called apartments, it is easier to debase mankind. That is more or less the logic of prisons; one might call them pre-prisons rather than apartments.[12]

However, despite all that, in that hostile environment, it turns out that man has not lowered his head. He has hung a picture of his boss on the wall, and on the shelves of his modest bookcase the works of that boss are in a place of honour, even though he might grumble about the government, make fun of the Minister of Foreign Affairs who is standing like a stork at the airport waiting for a delegation from North Korea to arrive, and get angry without missing a word of the eight o'clock news. But he need not do anything of that kind in order to be immovable. He can be just that when, in the middle of his miserable lodgings, he manages to tell his wife whom he loves, 'My dear, you're wonderful.'

Bureaux. Businesses. Editorial Offices. Public Halls. Amphitheatres, etc. It's easy to imagine how the fighting goes on in these places, how good retreats in the face of evil, or the other way round. Although both camps use the same language, everyone knows who is for the government and who is against it.

Faces. Bodies. In dictatorial regimes, faces and bodies often reveal exactly what is happening in people's minds under all circumstances. An unnatural whitish colour, a kind of sanctimonious puffiness, as it were, on the faces of functionaries (which you notice if you haven't seen them for some time, or when they've been promoted), reveals more reliably than any other clue that the man has finally gone over to the regime. A different rhythm in his walk, a new way of sitting down at table, of getting up, of saying certain things like, 'Well, what's the news, Comrades?', tends to prove the same thing.

The Countryside. Urban Design. The struggles and its incidents and reversals have often found remarkable expression. Lugubrious buildings, a vacant lot used as a dump right in the midst of a green expanse, the words, 'Party–Enver' inscribed in oil paint, high up. Dust, heat, desolation. And floating over everything, boredom.

Boredom is the hallmark of dictatorship. It's an infallible gauge, just as the colour of the earth or the movements of a needle on a dial reveal the presence of one or another substance. But boredom is also a boon companion, an ally of the dictatorship.

In what manner, with the help of what barometer, does the totalitarian state measure its decline? That is one of its mysteries. The fall of boredom on the market is in effect an alarm bell. (Comrades, what's going on? Why do all these young women and young men dress like that and smile like that? What is that blue colour on balconies?[13] Those love poems? That music? Have we forgotten the bourgeois revisionist encirclement?)

On these battlefields the struggles wax and wane continually. At the end of the fifties and the beginning of the sixties, the Club of the Writers' Union was so lively, so pleasant, that on one December day I flew three thousand kilomètres from Moscow to Tirana just to spend the evening and have dinner there.

Naturally that club could never have lasted. A foreign body among the clubs of the time, places that gave one the pip, with their graphs of socialist rivalry, their half-broken chairs, their meeting table covered with a dusty red cloth that seemed to be waiting for the next gathering (the next cruelty) so as to build up its health—the Writers' Union Club was closed some years later.[14]

But things did not always fall out like that. Just the opposite might happen. A handsome building or a pretty park would spring up suddenly among the various shades of grey. A touch of grandeur, of nobility, might cut across the monotonous scene. A novel, a concert. On one such occasion, in that ambience of politicized deaths (heroism at the borders of the nation, the ordeal by fire that saved our socialist patrimony, etc), a death that was far from ordinary (not to say dissident) made a great stir: a suicide because of love.

Faces were still the battlefield; beards and long hair were still the grand problem for the government—those young faces which resembled neither the pasty-faced devotion of the functionaries, nor the muscular rigidity of their official portraits. The regime feared the young as if they made up a secret conspiracy.

There were people who, in their apartments, removed the picture of the great leader and his interminable collected works, and exchanged those things for a chandelier, the icon of a saint, or a poster of the Beatles.

People who had seemed lost, body and soul, including leading politicians, police officers, or officially recognized artists, suddenly cracked.[15] Official mischief could no longer make headway in Albania. The fact is that the country was regressing to its origins. One fine day you noticed that, despite everything, some authentic values had in fact been created. The deafening noise of government propaganda, promoting false values, had a great effect upon real values because of the contrast. And these were not moral values only; they changed every area of social existence, including the government itself, carried along by the logic of life that had arisen suddenly in the midst of a long cycle of aberration, and particularly affected by the nation's thousand-year culture and, why not, by the genius of the race.

To reject those values, given the difficult circumstances in which they had been developed, would have been not merely unjust but inhuman.

In those times when wrong is in retreat, like a lion licking its wounds, and life takes courage again, the totalitarian regime feels the danger keenly. It prepares for a counter-attack.

It would like to take full advantage of the mechanism of fear, as in the past (the calm before the storm, the thunder announcing the plot, the flash of lightning), but times have changed. So it falls back on the good old method, disfiguring life once again. It understands that disfiguring life is the key to its own longevity, so it lets things drag along as before. Otherwise sleep will steal upon it, the masks will slip, and with them the stage props will fall.

In the new conditions that the government faces, disfiguring life becomes more and more difficult. To begin with, the brains of the leaders are too atrophied to find clever solutions to their problems. They can only do what they have learned to do, quoting Marx, because they feel that he is still their special preserve. And his order of the day, 'The true meaning of life is struggle,' could scarcely be more useful in a time like this. A theoretical justification, as it were, of the deterioration of the ordinary (which in this instance spells apathy), all in the name of revolutionary dynamism.[16]

Relying on Marx's teachings, the Party renews the slogan of revolutionizing life (how often have we heard it!), this time by mass action. In plain language, break the normal rhythm of life, and since most voluntary activity happens on Sunday, it means that the Party's first aim is the abolition of Sunday. Until now, no one had given it a thought, just as no one pays attention to the sun above his head.* But that day that you have lost makes you suddenly aware that Sunday is one of the pillars of normal life. The loss of it announces further losses to come. The anaesthesia that the totalitarian state used to administer by means of fear now has another object: to throw confusion into the succession of the days. You are mortified to have to devote yourself daily to sterile things, meetings, assemblies, political councils, mass activities and work, as the ancient Babylonians who had to dig canals, or the more ancient Egyptians who were forced to build useless pyramids—that is the goal that the regime aims at. In that way you have no time to think about anything. And when the people think of nothing, the government is happy.

That is the absurd, useless rhythm that kills the desire to work, and that succeeded in doing what used to be inconceivable: to make the peasant uninterested in working the land and raising cattle.

But even that fever cannot last as long as the government hopes.

---

* In Albanian, the word *Sunday* also comes from the word *sun*.

At the end of the second or the third week, resistance begins. ('They're taking Sunday away from us, too!') The defence of Sunday has something to do with the chandelier in the apartment, with the woman writing a love letter, with hundreds of other things that seem to have nothing to do with politics. And then, among those hundreds of things, suddenly we see the government and mankind in open battle. It takes place on the terrain that was wholly unexpected, the terrain of death. Having subjected life to so many massacres, the totalitarian state is seized with a sudden taste for the rites of death. For the first time it begins to suspect that it is powerless. The state, which had never stepped back from anything, steps back from death. We shall come to that in the last section of these notes.

. . . When, some days before these lines were written, far off, in France in the Loire Valley, I heard a recording of a mass in Shkodra performed by Dom Simon Jubani—the *Ave Maria* sung divinely by an Albanian—and the report that Muslims as well as Catholics had participated in restoring the great cathedral, I said to myself (probably with thousands of other Albanians), from this time forward they can pride themselves on having shown that they have not been conquered by Lenin's doctrine. And they have the right to feel even more proud to have said goodbye to the evil doctrine, not in accordance with that doctrine, but, on the contrary, in keeping with their own culture and their own civilization.

When all over Albania people were talking about that mass and the *Ave Maria*, a mass perhaps unparalleled anywhere in the world, in which Christians and Muslims had taken part, no doubt there were fanatical militants who said, gritting their teeth, 'They shouldn't have made any concessions!' Frightened by the absence of fear, the fear that had paralysed the nation, worse than the effect of opiates, surely there had been those who sighed, full of nostalgia for the time when the communist world seemed eternal.

'How have we gone astray and let them slip through our fingers?' That was what they must have been saying to themselves, at the very moment when the others, confronting them, must have been saying,

'How could we have foundered so entirely in that world? That Zauberberg,* how could we have borne it for so long?'

The more time passes, the more difficult it will be to answer these questions. At the moment it seems impossible, just as it seems impossible to judge that world from the outside. If any judgement were correct, it would amount to no more than the analysis of a nightmare. Other laws governed that world, laws that will seem incomprehensible later, like the laws that governed the universe before the Big Bang, and disappeared with it.

Whenever I remember my attempt to flee in the summer of 1962, one question torments me: how can I explain that, having been in Finland, I wanted to go to the Soviet Union and not to the West? Was I so indoctrinated, so much under the spell of opium?

But when I think of that time, I know at once that it was not so. In 1962 I had written the first chapters of *The Twilight of the Gods of the Steppe*; therefore I knew all that I needed to know about that world. I knew of Stalin's crimes, the disillusionment of the Russians with communism, their despair and boredom. I was pleased with the break between Albania and the Soviet Union, since the omnipresent USSR (Russian inventors, Russian literature, hymns to eternal friendship, etc) had begun to get on my nerves, as it had for most young people in the socialist camp. I had come to Prague after an excursion in Finland, which is to say a sojourn in a beautiful Western country, and to top it off, while V. Kilica and I were walking in Wenceslas Square, two young Czech girls, who had heard where we had just come from, said to us, 'Lucky you, now you're a capitalist country!'

I knew all about that. Despite everything, I had no hesitation about the choice I was making. From the first day to the last, I looked on that flight as a flight to the Soviet Union.

Later, the mere fact that I had thought about it would make me despair. It seemed to me that there was something fatal in that

---

* In German in the text, from the title of *The Magic Mountain* by Thomas Mann.

attraction. Were we citizens of a socialist country doomed to live out our days in that world? Perhaps that is why at the moment of going into exile, our legs, like those of a sleepwalker, like animals guided by instinct, take us blindly towards the zone of shadows.

Sometimes I think that I've found the answer, but it eludes me again. Sometimes it seems that the flight from socialism is more or less comparable to man's imaginary flight from the planet earth: it makes no difference that he has suffered there, no difference that he is disgusted with it. After all, there is no other place, no other planet that he is accustomed to.

Perhaps that is the heart of the enigma. While not yet an entire planet, it is no less than half of the planet that has become socialist. That's a lot. That's an enormous territory. The socialist countries together are larger than the moon. That's enough to make the force of attraction terrible, so that it might take a different direction, making compasses go crazy and causing invisible waves.

That the communist world, despite the criticisms it has always had to endure, has exercised a mysterious attraction is certainly irrefutable. In his play *The Roots are Stirring*, written and published in Rome in 1968, just after the closing of Albania's churches, Ernest Koliqi[*] imagines the day when the churches will be open again. In that work of fiction the reopening is to take place in the 1970s, the day after the overthrow of communism. Among the characters there is a young man, a writer whom the communists have not published, and therefore an ex-dissident. While the other characters are celebrating the fall of communism with great joy, the writer, who has perhaps more reason for rejoicing than they, seems dismayed. One of them scolds him: 'You, who have borne so much from the communists, why do you react this way? Has a longing for those times seized you so swiftly?'

That is an astonishing premonition, particularly if we take into

---

[*] An Albanian writer of the 1930s who sympathized with Italian fascism and fled to Rome after the installation of the communist regime in Albania.

account that this comes from Ernest Koliqi, a confirmed anti-communist. But when it comes to writers, one has to believe them.

Yes, paradoxical as that seems, the communist world is capable of inspiring a certain longing. Today that's hard to understand because people's feelings are still at fever pitch. The passion that condemns it for its good aspects as well as bad, drowns every other feeling. As it happens, there are people who think that, like any system under which millions of individuals have lived and died, that world too, which is certainly the sum of their faults and their merits, had a kind of internal balance, something that in ordinary human discourse is called their good and their bad sides. From that point of view, moreover, it suffices to mention the colossal intellectual riches that had seen the light during that period—a treasure that belongs now to all mankind, without which the century would have been the poorer. But that system has been so flattered, it has blown its own trumpet to such effect that it appears to have forfeited the right to have its good qualities recognized—those that the West has wisely and quietly borrowed in order to improve and invigorate itself. Nowadays, while the time of its funeral is at hand, the time in which the worldly life of the defunct is remembered only for his good traits, everyone appears to be pitiless when it comes to judging communism. Well, then, even if the life of social systems hardly resembles that of human beings, it is nevertheless right to remember the lesson of the ancient Greeks about going to excess. Exaggeration ensures that the right migrates to one's adversaries. Communism, in the barbarous form into which it had developed by the end of this century, the end of this millennium, had markedly violated that law, and the law is avenging itself now. The only possibility of its revival resides in a new violation of that law, committed by its adversaries this time. An exaggerated severity will provoke a new transfer of the right, replacing it on the other side, and it can revive in this way, more menacing, in a form even more detestable than the old one.

There has been much debate about the causes of the rise of communism and its expansion; about the suffering, the dreams, the

Utopian perspectives, the human hopes; about equality, happiness, justice, a better world, etc. But the last word on all this has yet to be said, and it may be that it is still too soon to speak of it.

We are not far enough away to grasp and render a judgement on the historical landscape in which communism developed. The record of events is too fresh to be gauged with any precision. We have no way of knowing its victories and defeats, since the reasons just mentioned mean that the eye is bound to see amiss—so much so that where communism has triumphed it may seem to have been vanquished and, inversely, where it has appeared invulnerable it may in fact have been beaten.

All we know thus far is a single performance, its very first appearance on history's stage, preceded by its phantom (the spectre that Marx and Engels mention in the first line of *The Communist Manifesto*). We have no experience of the second phantom, the one that may come after it has been expelled, the true one, the spectre of tragedy, the one that threatens to make the world tremble much more than the first. We know the idols of its beginnings, Marx and Engels, but we know nothing about the others who may appear in the sequel. At bottom, we do not know how many times it may appear and take its place in one form or another on this planet.

Its propensity to spread itself all over the world can be seen without question in its attempts to become ever more absolute, ever more self-sufficient, which amounts to what might be called its tendency towards universalization. Its triumph over half of the earth has made that dream only too plausible.

That 'new world', as communism calls itself, is of the same kind, whether it spreads over the endless territory of Russia or over a smaller region like Albania. If we examine it with a telescope to determine its extent, or with a microscope to determine the nature of its tissue, we are still in the same universe.

Moreover, like every system that tends towards absolutes, communism makes a point of having its own heaven, its own earth, its own hell. It has its gods of the highest rank, Marx, Engels, Lenin, but other gods, too, of a second and even a third rank. And it has demi-gods as well, idols, heroes, etc. When quarrels arise or internal polemics, it calls upon its gods as absolute judges. These are infallible, and the citations drawn from their doctrines are regarded as the highest law. These cannot be set aside or criticized. At most, one might possibly differ with a deity of the second or third order, that is to say, an idol; but the highest divinities, never. They represent the summit and the base of that world. Their prestige is such that even dissidents are confounded by them. No, you may not go beyond the threshold. Stalin possibly, Mao possibly, but Lenin—hands off. To regard Lenin as a colossus of revolution, but at the same time to have any reservations about him—to say, for example, that while displaying the most delicate feelings on seeing a fox killed (as millions of children learn at school), and representing him as a lover of foxes but one devoid of pity for human beings is heresy pure and simple. To call attention to the fact that he did not much care for intellectuals, that he conceived of formulas at once Byzantine and mean, like so-and-so is with us, so-and-so is not with us; even better, to say that despite all the fuss that has been made over his weakness for Beethoven's *Apassionata* and for that mediocre story by Jack London, *Love of Life* (what a comparison!), he did not understand a thing about literature and it was apparent in his book, *Party Organization and Party Literature*, one of the dreariest essays ever written, would certainly earn you a denunciation as an agent of the CIA.

Engels has a special position among the three classic founders. He represents, as it were, the good-natured tendency; he is a pre-figuration of the technocratic communist leaders (Zhou Enlai, for example), the fringe type whom the liberals can bank on, those who cherish their illusions—generally speaking, the intellectuals. That is their consolation, the balm applied to their bruised spirits. (Oh, Engels, how different he is, so generous, so noble!) But to say that, aside from having a generous spirit, and despite the noble character of his views—qualities that are hard to dispute—it is one of his ideas about the character of letters that destroyed literature for a century in a number of countries; and particularly to say that the Party spirit, according to Lenin's barbarous article and Engels' typology of literature, was worse than the Mongol hordes in its effect on art and letters, would shock everybody, including your friends.

And then there is the grandest, the first of the three, Marx. For long decades the cult of Marx could not be questioned. He was an undoubted genius. Millions of people, among whom were persons with open minds, came into the world and left it with the unshakeable conviction that his genius was absolute and infallible. To rise and say that this genius, nevertheless, had a serious fault was worse than suicide. But that failing of Marx was no ordinary matter. It was one that brought about crimes and annihilated millions of human destinies. A man whose entire life was preoccupied with social upheaval cannot be excused for having forgotten a fundamental law of humanity, that law mentioned earlier, discovered by the ancient Greeks two thousand, five hundred years ago: the migration of right. We might pardon any other philosopher, but not this one. That law should have revealed itself to him on every page that he wrote about the class struggle. One need not be a genius to find it. To discover that every overthrow is attended by the danger of revenge pushed too far, revenge that engenders acts of violence and more vengeance. All of the ancient literature of Greece is founded upon that. We encounter that truth in the legends of every people; a thousand years ago the rude Albanian mountaineers set down that law among the foundations of their own Code. Marx never mentions it anywhere. He is blind to it. More accurately, he does not wish to see that law, like the man who looks away so as not to be witness to a crime.

These, then, are the primary gods of that world. The members of the Politburo in all socialist countries have aspired in secret to a similar cult, a kind of sub-Olympus. In the Soviet Union it began with baptizing cities with their own names. They wanted to show that they were the peers of Peter the Great, the equals of the tzars. In Albania, Hysni Kapo, one of the secretaries of the Central Committee, luxuriates in a bust much larger than that of Ismail Qemal, who founded the Albanian state in 1912. While the complete works of classic Albanian literature have not yet been published, the 'complete works' of the members of the Politburo, their speeches, are in print, and those 'works' have no value whatsoever. In the Albanian Encyclopedic Dictionary, the members of the Politburo take up much too much space and are shown in larger portraits than those of the great figures of Albanian history and culture. Thus the former member of a cooperative, Lenka Çuko, now a member of the Politburo, takes up more space than a cultural genius like Fan Noli, President of the Albanian Republic in 1924. The same is true of the former sawyer, P. Miska, or former wheelwrights, or former professional drivers, etc, all of whom have become leaders not because of their revolutionary record, but because they were elevated under socialism, at a time when even the Albanian university (where most of them had never set foot) was turning out administrators in all areas.

It is painful to think that the cultural level of the leaders in 1978 was incomparably lower than that of the Albanian government of the League of Prizren a hundred years earlier in 1878.

It's easy to see that the new group of leaders, aware of being below the level and dignity of the Albanian people—which had perhaps developed to excess the cult of elitism and of the noble traditions of the leaders of the past—were by instinct in conflict with the nation. For that reason, when it came to abolishing values, those people who had never been zealous about anything became zealots at once. They hurried to destroy the educational system, to muzzle publication, to sterilize arts and letters. They were especially eager to strike at the chief figures in the realms of culture and the sciences, their favourite targets.

That explains why people were attacked for having a 'propensity to make themselves conspicuous', and 'the arrogance of privileged characters', which led to 'the necessity for writers and artists to mingle with the people, soil their hands with mud', etc; these bromides, whether handed down by Lenin or Mao Zedong, were particularly dear to the new leaders.

The movement to introduce a different intellectual landscape into the socialist university was a feature of the struggle that the regime undertook on all levels in order to retrain the nation to its own liking. In a word, the intention was to lower the standards of the nation, and align them with their own.

To accomplish that, it was necessary to create a whole system of idols and heroes to replace distinguished personages, the stars of the old order. But, while replicas of Stakhanovitch were being created in Albania, the country failed to produce monsters like Li-feng in China or Pavlik Morozov in the Soviet Union (the pioneer who denounced his father), which showed that the Albanian nation did not bend easily.

In the autumn, before the November holidays, every district sent candidates to a centre to be chosen as heroes or idols: the blind who were champion marksmen(!), workmen who had been crippled in trying to rescue a tractor, literary people who gladly surrendered their earnings to the state. The selections took place at that centre, and they chose the stars.

The fascination exerted by those invalids upon many functionaries must not have been foreign to their own personal universe, to their complexes and weaknesses. Albanian society as a whole did not restrict itself to ignoring the new idols, but jeered mercilessly. For example, a blind man, F. Çela, though he had visited Enver Hoxha, was the target of so many jibes that it grew painful to everyone, so much so that the press stopped all discussion of it.

From that mania for idols one can deduce the general character of the officials. Incompetence and ignorance were the qualities most sought after. Naturally, the dictatorship was not so foolish as to use that vocabulary. In accordance with custom, they employed certain euphemisms in order to advance the cause. Incompetence was labelled 'concern for the question at hand', ignorance 'class membership'. It was not accidental that for many years the patroness of these officials was Lenka Çuko, the most ignorant member of the Politburo. She and the person directly in charge of the administrative group within the Central Committee, M. Bisha* (what a name!), an

---

* In Albanian, a wild beast.

obscure man who held his post for twenty-five years, had in their hands the files and the fate of the elite of the country.[17]

People began to wonder, more and more: Why is it that in Albania, the more diplomas of higher education, the more the educational level of the administrators is lowered. To counter that, the Party, attentive mother of the administrators, takes steps to spare her children such dishonour. It establishes the V.I. Lenin School, offering a lightweight course on the Soviet model of the Komsomol courses, but officially a part of the university. In this way, after having gone through Purgatory, all the administrators wake up one fine morning equipped with higher education. That was the solution for the pressing problem of the administrators.

One can imagine the character of the confraternity (or guild) that this army of administrators represents. They must not simply resemble one another in their mode of reasoning, but in every trait: their sense of humour, how they express themselves, how they work, how they dress.

From time to time, that army felt the need to rid itself of certain 'professors', as does the rude Mafia in Sicily. It raised the tone of the place and allowed them to cure their complexes. (Now that we have professors among us, no one can say that . . .) But the professors had to be of a certain stamp—to be on our side, as Lenin put it. Professor Eqrem Çabej, for example, was absolutely the wrong man for the purpose, as were others who, like himself, worked with genuine creativity and showed signs of distinction, something that in his case was interpreted as 'arrogance'. Equally unadaptable were some talented people who were also naive, like the brilliant old economist whose name I prefer not to mention, and who, having been summoned for three months at a stretch by the Council of Ministers as an economic consultant, had to be admitted to a psychiatric establishment for another three months to recover.

The professors cherished by the state were of a special kind. Hatred of the intellectuals, as exemplified in the treatment accorded Professor Sofo Lazri by his colleagues, was a much-prized quality.

When they climb the ladder to power, the professors may show good as well as bad conduct. But experience suggests that the good they can do in their positive actions is much more limited than the evil they can cause through their bad ones. An ill-disposed 'professor' is ten times more dangerous than an ignoramus because he has a trump card, his credibility. He has risen to power as a liberal. He has accepted that name, and he has even endured its drawbacks. At times he has declared himself in favour of positive steps like accelerating the talks with the Federal Republic of Germany, or with the United States, or accepting the Helsinki Declaration. But from the day that he suddenly changes his position, when after those good preliminary negotiations with the Germans he does what he can to torpedo them, capable of doing the same thing tomorrow with the Americans or in the matter of the Helsinki Charter, he is the personification of a genuine plague. No conservative coven could deliver such mortal thrusts. (Since the professor has advised us to bury the negotiations, throw the treaty into the fire, what are we waiting for? Since the professor himself has said that the dictatorship should show its teeth to the intellectuals, that means we've had it up to here. Strike without asking questions!)

That cohort of administrators, supported by thousands of Party militants, used to dominate, or more accurately believed that it dominated, the communist world. For in that universe, just as with feelings of guilt, fear or a host of other things, power itself was expressed in a particular way. This was not due simply to those instruments through which it was exerted: the machinery of violence, the manipulation of language, the subversion of morality, or the recourse to mystification—like the slogan, 'The stronger the dictatorship, the greater the liberty,' ascribed to Albania; to Mexico, the world prize for nourishment! etc—but equally to the fact that that world, as we saw above, is a disfigured world. The hocus pocus of its beginnings (the subordinate figures who were the true bosses, the double-dealing of the Party bureaux . . .) has brought forth its fruits.

In my novel, *The Palace of Dreams*, though I set out with no analogy in mind, involuntarily, in the very first pages, I sketched one facet of that world. A world that is very much a dream world. A world apart, ambivalent, that makes me think of a word in old Albanian, *i damun*, which has several meanings: separated, driven away, isolated, accursed, devil. (According to some linguists the words 'devil', 'son'* and 'Adam' may be derived from the first.)

One can imagine that in such a world, as a result of dismemberment and division, breaches of outward appearance, and of mystifications and delusions, our way of seeing changes completely. I remember quite clearly that from the age of thirteen or fourteen, when for the first time I became vaguely conscious of political life, I was absolutely convinced that Stalin was nothing more than a nice old man who had no power at all, and who had to be on show with a little smile on his face. I would be exaggerating if I said that I pitied him. Sometimes, also without pity (probably because he was much younger), I saw Enver Hoxha in much the same light. Curiously enough, I was to feel that way later, when I was a university student, and even more curiously, my friends felt something of that kind about him, too. But in this context, the adverb 'curiously' is certainly too weak. There are discussions that take this form: Who is the real leader, who has power, who does not, who is 'strong' and who is not; this is our daily fare and fate. One of the foundations of power is its mystery.

Here are some fragments from among the thousands that make up this mosaic and can testify to it.

The year is 1973. Ramiz Alia's office. Himself. The head of the press, P. Mitrojorghi. Me, summoned in haste. Another person whose name is mentioned (M. Verli, Editor-in-Chief of *The Voice of Youth*) is not present.

Ramiz Alia shows me the journal, *The Voice of Youth*, in which there is a dreadful review—the third one to appear—of my novel *The Great Winter*. It is nine o'clock in the morning; I've not yet seen the article. Ramiz Alia seems nervous, distracted. I don't understand why they summoned me. The press chief has an icy expression.

---

* In Albanian, the word for *son* is *djalë*; the word for *devil* is *djall*.

'I told him to put a stop to that campaign,' he said, 'but Verli has betrayed me.'

A surprising turn of phrase, unheard of in that office: 'has betrayed me.'

'Don't worry about it,' Ramiz Alia says to me, still looking absent.

I leave them. I go outside. I can't make head or tail of it. What is this monkey business? Alone in the café, I turn it around and around in my head. There is something odd going on. Little by little that something begins to take shape in my mind. I'm helped by my experience of life in that world, by all that I had heard there, and had felt confusedly until now. We were four characters in that affair. Two of them must know the truth, or at least one of them. The other two, no. So two were masters of the situation, and the other two were the turkeys in the farce. As paradoxical as it may seem, it was clear that the two losers were Ramiz Alia and me. I, since I was the author of the book; he, as Chief of Propaganda, exposed to criticism for several weeks.

Seventeen years have gone by since then, and to this day I do not know who received the secret order to launch that campaign, or from whom. Which of the two functionaries had been laughing up his sleeve while sympathizing with our concern—we, the two losers who thought we represented something, one as a member of the Politburo and the other as a famous writer, when in reality we were nothing at all? I believe that even today, Ramiz Alia though he be, still does not know the truth of the story. Of the four of us, one, Ramiz Alia, has become President, I am in France, the Press Director has retired, and the Editor-in-Chief lies in his grave where, it seems to me, he has taken the secret.

Another scene. The year is 1978. At the office of the First Secretary of the Party Committee of Tirana. Three people: the First Secretary, Simon Stefani, his deputy, Xhelil Gjoni, and me, summoned in haste.

Sombre atmosphere. But I have in my pocket a passport that allows me to go abroad, and in that world such a document has miraculous powers. The more so since it had been issued on the direct order of Enver Hoxha who, after five years of hesitation, had just authorized the publication of *The Great Winter* in France. I was going to Paris to see if someone had made a comment on the book's cover that might be politically embarrassing.

'We have asked you to come here to inform you that your sister is saying bad things about the government,' Simon Stefani says gravely.

'That doesn't surprise me,' I say.

My answer must have surprised them. In fact, I knew very well that she was criticizing the regime. I had suggested that she hold her tongue, if only for my sake.

'If she were not your sister she would be behind bars.'

'I don't know what to say.'

'Your brother rails at the government, too,' Xhelil Gjoni puts in.

'That's not true. My brother does nothing of the kind.'

They look at each other.

'It's possible that our information is mistaken,' Simon Stefani says while shuffling his papers. 'But as for your sister, there is no doubt about it.'

'I can imagine my sister saying things. My brother, never.'

I leave the office. On my way home I think about telephoning my mother and my aunts, to warn them. I'm really annoyed with my sister, especially since, if I understand what is going on, she's been discussing my private life to satisfy the curiosity of her friends. I'm in a rage, and decide to tell her not to set foot in my house until she learns to hold her tongue.

I feel the passport in my pocket, and I tell myself, 'Idiots, you think you can frighten me.'

And, after my departure, they must certainly have said, 'That idiot! He thinks that since he is a well-known writer with a passport in his pocket, he has nothing to worry about.'

A few hundred yards from there, in another office, a third person who knew much more than we did must surely have been saying, 'What a bunch of idiots, on one side and on the other.'

Yet another scene. A brief epilogue. One year later. Once more in Ramiz Alia's office. I had been asked to come, I don't remember why. As I was leaving he said, 'Oh, I almost forgot something. Comrade Enver doesn't remember who told him that you are still mad at your sister, but he asked me to tell you that you must not be so unyielding.'

I leave, dumbfounded. As a friend of mine had told me, though my own file was inadequate, apparently my sister's file at the Sigurimi was really terrifying. What she had said about Enver Hoxha in her circle of women friends could have cost her her life. So why was he so solicitous about her?

My mother, trusting her intuition, had a simple explanation: Enver Hoxha had an unmarried sister, and whenever there was an old maid in question his heart melted.

The double aspect of that world, its secrets, its two anomalous faces, makes mystification natural. Sometimes it's very difficult to analyse. The mystification, too, has a double character: the Great Mystification, which is general and a matter of principle; and the small mystification, a banal and everyday affair. Each contributes to the other. The result is a third form that can be classed as a perfect synthesis: self-mystification.

There has been much discussion of the Great Mystification, the presentation of things in diluted form, disseminated through newspapers, television, public gatherings, speeches. The most democratic system in history. The happiest nation in the world. One hundred per cent electoral participation. A hundred per cent of votes in favour of the regime, etc. And there has been much discussion of the daily mystification: disinformation, calumny, corruption. Now and then, the border that separates these things is obscured in the mist.

Here is a significant event that shows the intricate relations between the greater and lesser mystification. The Ninth Party Congress. The one that renders hope vain, and is called with ostentation 'The Congress of Continuity'. A delegate takes the floor, a woman who works as a paediatrician in Elbasan. In a solemn voice she announces to the Congress that throughout the previous year there has not been a single case of infant mortality in Elbasan. The Congress is exultant. It cheers the speaker. Two weeks later I receive a letter: Go to the cemetery in Elbasan. Just glance at the inscriptions on the graves and you will understand, given the dates of death for the babies, how that doctor lied.

By that time the Congress had adjourned, but I couldn't help imagining someone bursting into the hall, bent over by the weight of the gravestones. And I think, 'Lord, how many gravestones must we bring to serve as documentary evidence?'

In that world, mystification grows easier and easier to launch, and more and more acceptable. Some officials know when they have been misled, but they don't give a damn about it. They fool others in the very same way. It comes to the point that they don't even hide their approval of such tactics, and when they say, 'Give me all the information,' for the most part they are thinking, 'Mislead me as well as you can.'

In that way production statistics are falsified, as are the numbers of the unemployed, of political prisoners, of the proportion of Catholics, etc. Falsified data are given about working conditions, commerce, prison life, lawsuits, discussions with foreign delegations, and even about the temperature according to the meteorological bulletins (so as not to sow panic?).

The example of the hoax perpetrated by the paediatrician in Elbasan is macabre, but there are others that are even more diabolical, like the feigned message from Mladonov. After the fall of Jivkov, Sofo Lazri, the President's adviser, travelled to Bulgaria on the pretext of improving relations between the two countries. At the very moment he returned, bearing what was claimed to be a verbal message from Mladonov to Ramiz Alia, Mladonov fell from grace in Bulgaria. Sofo Lazri transmitted the message—that no one can ever authenticate. It is more than surprising. According to Lazri, Mladonov wanted to tell the Albanian leader: Don't be in any hurry to bring about reforms, for you are likely to regret it, like me.[18]

Sofo Lazri, whom the Swedish writer Jan Myrdal described as 'the administrator with the Vietnamese psychology', is the man in charge of Albanian foreign affairs and the instigator of ignoble and calamitous friendships with Cuba, Libya, and North Korea. It can be said without exaggeration that five hundred years ago, in 1460, Albania had a far more respectable foreign policy and was better informed. The direction of that policy is clear from the reports of the chancellery of Pal Engieli, at that time the First Secretary of Skanderberg. The names of the countries with which Albania had ties—Italy, Spain, the Vatican, England, France, the German principalities—appear in most of the archives of the period.

Like fear, the purpose of mystification is to conceal everything, and thus to reign over everything. Put another way, if it breaks out in one place it is in danger of turning things upside down somewhere else. But in order to achieve complete control it must enter into a phase that has been most carefully devised, the phase of self-mystification.

That is a sort of drug by means of which the totalitarian regime attempts to keep its servitors in a state of permanent excitement (ecstasy). Hysterical activity, incomprehensible directives, bursts of enthusiasm, follies of every order, are the usual consequences of self-mystification.

There are also events or institutions that turn out to be the full panoply of deceit. The governmental organ whose mission is to deal with the requests and the provisioning of the administrative force, the so-called 'Welcoming Bureau', is perhaps the most nauseating emanation of the socialist system. The hoaxes in that arena are extraordinarily complex. The principles of communist doctrine (class struggle, perfection of the administration against the class enemy, etc) run cheek by jowl with the most commonplace lies (illnesses invented as a pretext for going abroad, the disappearance of bills and invoices . . . in the name of vigilance!—in a word, classic, authentic fraud, and a sprinkling of Marxism-Leninism.)[19]

Another example. This time, auto-mystification mixed with

hysteria. The scene: my apartment in Tirana, 25 October 1990, after the revelation of my departure for France. In the afternoon, just after the announcement of that news, the police arrive; they allow no one to enter or leave. Inside is my eighty-year-old mother, almost blind, and my sister. One can imagine their fright. One of my aunts, coming to bring them something to eat, is searched at the door. The food and the crockery are inspected too.

Why? What is the meaning of that? No one can possibly understand it.

Then come investigators, representing the public prosecutor's office, who want to conduct a search. They turn everything upside down. Surely they have been waiting long years for such a triumph. They sniff around everywhere, in my study, the bedroom, the drawers, in all the most personal nooks and crannies of the household.

One asks again, what for? What are they looking for so zealously? If you were to ask them, they could not possibly say. In fact, they are looking for nothing. Trained all their lives to deal with plots that never existed, dangers completely fabricated, fictions—it seems quite normal to go ferreting around under the eyes of two distressed women in order to find nothing.

Eventually, they seize six boxes of manuscripts, and then leave. Somewhere, in another office, they are concocting an official bulletin on my 'desertion'. In an interview with *The New York Times*, I suggested that the communiqué appeared to have been written by a gangster, but it was much worse than that. In my declaration,* I stated clearly that I would return to Albania as soon as genuine democratization had been achieved, the intention and the hope that I still have today as I write these lines. In order to avoid any misunderstanding, I had emphasized that I meant to return after the establishment of democracy, and not the day after some catastrophe—and I wish for it now with all my heart just as on the day that I wrote those words.

---

* See pages 113–114.

But the hurtful, brutal tone of the communiqué in the Albanian press[20] clearly showed that there was a reactionary group in the country that would brook no suggestion of my returning. Adam Demaçi claimed to have information that the Albanian government had known that Ismail Kadare intended to flee, but had done nothing to keep me from doing it. Though it is hard for me to subscribe wholly to that thesis, his remark was at bottom quite true. They had certainly told themselves, what luck that he fled! May he never set foot here again!

It's easy to imagine their remarks: We knew who he was, but no one would listen to us. We warned the Party so many times . . . So many times we suggested that he . . . Unfortunately . . .

To keep clear views in a labyrinth of distorting mirrors is not easy. All the citizens of a communist country, from the street-sweepers to the Head of State, need not blush to confess that during their life, they suffered at least one attack of madness. Zone 'M' differs, no doubt, according to the differences among people: the attack may have lasted for years, for months, and in rare instances, for only a few weeks. The authors of these lines had noticed that the biography of anyone, including himself, could scarcely be exhaustive unless it included the phenomenon of Zone 'M'.

It is an extremely difficult task, the more so because in that world one cannot lose one's reason *all alone*. The madness generally strikes like a wave that carries away whole layers of society, and entire generations.

The images refracted in that universe, its tensions, its psychoses, often make people's relations disconcerting. Often, they cannot understand one another. Imagine how impenetrable they must be to a foreign onlooker.

Different viewpoints, different objectives can lead to tragic misunderstandings. Hasty judgements made by outsiders on the morality or courage of the inhabitants of that world can often arise from mere superficiality, but there are instances that can only be imputed to a kind of carefully veiled sadism, not to say an appetite for criminality.

Those who would give lessons do not always examine their own conduct before setting out to preach to the people who live in that other world. The abnegation of some persons who live in the socialist universe can really go as far as self-sacrifice. They do not ask for protection, because the concept of protection does not exist there. In that regard, the abolition of lawyers in Albania in 1967 was most significant; the purpose was to emphasize that anyone whom the regime meant to attack was alone, and therefore doomed.

When in 1975 I was forbidden to publish anything for a fairly long period, my writing was already known in Europe. My books had been translated in some fifteen countries, but no one thought to ask, What has happened to that writer? Is he still alive? Why haven't we seen any new stories by him?

I didn't expect protection in my own country, for I knew that was impossible, but I thought I might hope for some attention abroad, and I waited for it anxiously. It didn't happen, and then I understood that the regime could strangle me and no one would care.

At the end of a meeting in 1982, at which I was again severely criticized, the writer N.J. told me as I was leaving the hall that Neshat Tozaj, whom I didn't know at the time, had wanted to rise to my defence, but another comrade and he had prevented it. He told me how they had intervened (things had gone so far that M.V. had to force him to sit down—you get the picture?). As for me, I listened in astonishment.

Most sincerely, and to their great surprise, I told them that, given the circumstances, they had done the right thing. I was sure that my being defended would not have helped at all, while Neshat Tozaj would have doomed himself, and his novel *The Knives* would never have seen the light of day.

Much has been said about courage under dictatorship; the matter is one about which people have not been chary with their advice. Moralizing has been popular in the cafés of Paris and Vienna, and is no doubt a comfort. I've met a number of those orators when they came to Albania. At the end of a week's sojourn, their appearance and their tone were quite different; one of them, in a fit of sincerity, confessed to me that, while he knew that foreigners were sheltered from any danger, he had escaped neither fear nor deep distress.

Others, one's compatriots, also lecture you. But they do it too late, when the dictatorship begins to soften, and they forget that they were the people who once filled the public halls to sing its glory. To beat one's breast after the fact, when the dictatorship has lost its teeth, playing at dissidence to show one's courage, to pride oneself on having been the first to express criticism, to have gone furthest in denouncing this or that, to accuse one another, to throw mud at one another, to berate oneself, etc, is all a tiny sample of the post-dictatorial uproar in a number of East European countries. In all that cacophony, it often happens that the real opponents of dictatorship, those who for long years had been mining its foundations, are thrust aside and forgotten.

Among those who, for one reason or another, have not led a productive life (including, of course, people who have been abused by the dictatorship), there are some who feel that the time has come for revenge. They can think of nothing but assuaging their rancour and would destroy the lives of those who, in their eyes, may have had some connection with their suffering. They don't stop to remember that they are dealing with the teachers who taught their children, the architects who built their homes, the doctors who saved their lives.

They have forgotten all that, they want vengeance here and now—that is, to cry shame upon them, to ruin their careers, and, if possible, to lay hands on their houses.[21]

Even a fragmentary sketch of that universe would be incomplete if one did not mention the wind that blows upon him night and day, the wind of hate. In opening their bag, the classics of Marxism-Leninism have filled the world with that hatred, much more than the Aeolus of the ancient Greeks.

In their works and in their speeches one cannot find any mention of the pestilential stench that accompanies every social revolution, like the wind that often follows the earthquake. No counselling of moderation to the victors drunk with victory, no warning. On the contrary: an exhortation to fan the flames.

Hatred has become a science. We must learn to hate scientifically. These sinister suggestions are not imaginary. They have been fashionable slogans in the Soviet Union. There is even a story by Sholokhov entitled *The Science of Hatred* (*Nauka Nyenavisti*).

When, from the Russian steppes the winds of hate burst over Albania, one of its greatest tragedies befell that nation. For a thousand and more years she had been trying—and she had succeeded—to keep a lid on the powder-keg of hatred. In the ancient Code were laws that, upon first sight, might seem positively disconcerting: when a man killed to take vengeance, he was obliged to take part in his victim's funeral. The murderer must show no sign of arrogance. He was required not only to attend the funeral feast, but to sit at table and eat with the members of the enemy clan. These laws, paradoxical as they seem, followed an internal logic. Together with other provisions (forbidding contact with the victim's body, etc), they were features of a system that restrained hatred.

Marxist doctrine has not only abolished all systems of that sort, but it has gone a long way in the opposite direction. It built a factory to produce its poison day and night. And it was certainly the most efficient factory in all the communist world. Its engines turned unceasingly. Hatred was one of the foundations upon which dictatorship was based. If it were ever to slacken, the entire structure would be in danger.[22] The antidotes—pardon, repentance, apology, pity, religion—were rooted out wherever they appeared. The regime only became more resolute.

Hatred was sown everywhere, among young women in the textile industry, among academicians, bureaucrats, students, peasants, artists—and everywhere the people resisted it. They were the countrymen of Mother Teresa, and not by chance.

The signs of contrition shown from time to time by the President of the Writers' Union, Dritero Agolli, whom the regime forced for many years to attack me, were enough to make me forgive everything. My friends said, 'You are not naturally soft-hearted, so why do you make apologies for him? You don't need his help. On the contrary, he needs yours.' But this was not a matter of need. I forgave him because I admired his talent, because in this cruel world we were two monks of the same order, and above all, because I valued contrition, a very rare trait in the socialist world. In his case it showed itself in the most unexpected ways. One night in November of 1983, during a time of much tension between us, we were returning from Paris, both members of a small delegation of five writers. At that time he was at the height of his power, and I was enduring one of my darkest years. On the way home, we spent one night in Budapest. After dining with our ambassador, on which occasion he drank a bit more than was necessary, we went to our hotel to sleep. As a member of the Central Committee of the Party, he was entitled to have a room for himself; the rest of us were to sleep two to a room. About one o'clock in the morning, someone knocked at the door. It was Dritero Agolli with his hair rumpled. 'Listen,' he said. 'Go and sleep in my room, it's better. I'll sleep here. You know, you're a little squeamish, but me, I'm used to getting along without comfort. I know it bothers you to be in a double room. Go ahead, sleep well. You've had enough trouble . . .'

Those words, which might seem commonplace to many people, were to me of greater value than all his speeches in plenary sessions. It was one of those signs—one among hundred thousand—that evil would not bring down my country. So many human relationships had deteriorated. So many souls had been pillaged, and had dried up. It looked like the history of the Sahara desert. The wasting away, the retreat of the vegetation at the fateful advance of the sands. From the time they tore down the posters advertising the evening dances, the *soirées dansantes*, in 1945, and then the closing of the churches, and the suppression of lawyers in 1967, dozens of similar measures were promulgated, all to the same end, to dilute the stream of life, or, to be more exact, to devitalize it.

But, as I have mentioned, during its rise, the dictatorship of the proletariat encountered an unforeseen obstacle: the rites of death.

The classics of Marxism had provided certain suggestions on that subject. But given the fact that those rites were bound up with human nature, which those classics so misunderstood, their teachings were poverty-stricken. In closing the churches and mosques, and in forbidding crosses on graves, the Stalinists imagined they were getting rid of funerary rites. And they went still further. Even as they imagined they had invented a 'new life' and a 'new man', they imagined that they could also invent a 'new death'. They couldn't shout it from the rooftops, but they did their utmost to introduce those things as customary. The 'new death' differed from ordinary death in that the end was different. Either a man died in battle with the enemies of the revolution, or he perished in the flames, or froze in the snow for the sake of socialist property. Books and films were full of that kind of death, while the usual passing due to illness or old age seemed no longer to exist. To lend substance to the scene, they tried to replace the priests and *hodjas* with a representative of the Front who could, at funerals, replace the usual religious prayers with ridiculous speeches about the deceased's loyalty to the Party, to the fulfilment of the Plan, etc.[23]

But the Stalinists soon discovered that to disfigure death was much more difficult than to disfigure life. The old rites refused to capitulate. The Stalinist assault, which had destroyed private property, human warmth, marriage and justice, beat a retreat when confronted by those customs. And the people began to understand what great spiritual riches were represented by those immemorial rites.

People gathered in their houses and apartments to offer condolences; they drank coffee together on the eve of the funeral, and they talked things over as men and women had done for a thousand years. And the light of the funeral candles brought the dawn of the first alternative. There, socialist optimism was strangled, the slogans of the Party Congress ridiculed. There hatred subsided, as did the class struggle; in their place, the philosophy of life and of pardon sprang up anew.

And another extraordinary thing happened. People began to speak normally again. Deformed and pitilessly dried out, ordinary speech awakened as if from a coma. People used the age-old expressions:

'It's God's will . . ., all of us go to that last, long home . . ., the deceased . . .', etc. Then, just as in speech, everything returned to normal. Suddenly the crude and miserly doctrine, and its classics together with it, looked faded, untrue, insignificant.

It was not by chance that in February 1990 the mortality rate shot up in Tirana. Funeral rites became again what they had always been, a necessary part of history, revived this time in the clubs and the circles of the opposition.

As if to illustrate the change in a spectacular way, thousands of candles lit the two great cemeteries of the capital.

In meeting after meeting, the Party Secretary of Tirana, Pirro Kondi, struggled like a devil in the font. What should we do about the cemeteries? Send the militants to snuff out the candles? Send the police, the young pioneers?

Paradoxically, death had come to help the living. Under that banner it was easier to root out the evil.

However, in these changing times, there is still an evil more dangerous than any other: hatred.

The winds of hate . . . the piercing whistles that pervaded all of that period. On the day that it dies down even a little, in the heavenly expanse that will bring forth the day when it ceases entirely, our ears, all of our being, so unaccustomed to love, may feel pained. How far from us then will sound the roll of drums, the hubbub of parades, the clamour of meetings, the hymns and the threats. But then, at that critical moment, at the hinge between two epochs, when we think we have said goodbye to evil, the buzzing of hate might again make itself heard, more fatal than ever.

Of all the troubles of this world, hate bids fair to be the one that most wilfully tries to pass from one period to the next.

That would mean the return of human tragedy. In its wake would follow all the rest: bloody revenge, the screams of the vanquished, torment, death. Tired of the drama newly begun, the nation would give itself up that much sooner. And everything would go on as before.

Finding the method, the dam, the dyke capable of holding back the flood of hatred and all other agents of contagion in a given era, is a problem which never fails to perplex even the boldest spirits.

Today in 1990, ten years before the end of the second millennium, when the human race is hoping to enter the third with some greater sense of nobility, several countries have just come away from dictatorship, and finding that dyke is for them a primordial obsession.

The secrets of the Egyptian pyramids or the labyrinth of Crete were carefully kept, but the secrets of that dyke are more hidden still.

A barrier against evil, a sterile bandage, a vaccine, a no man's land, a clean break . . . but it is in vain that we search for such correctives, because the remedy is within each of us. The crowd milling around in the streets and the public squares during the troubled days when the dictatorship is tottering carries within itself both catastrophe and the means to avert it.

How to explain these things to them, how to calm them? . . . I'm writing the last lines of these notes in the month of December [1990]. Outside my window, the ground is covered with frost. But after I'd heard the news that party pluralism had been adopted in Albania yesterday, the rime looked to me like the white shimmer of a wedding; then, with the report of renewed violence, that white is spattered with blood. From far away, my country, where the troubles of transition have now begun, sends me its pain.[24]

Sombre thoughts assail me. It's December again, and I think of what happened a year ago in Romania. Had I said that the fate of Romania, predicted so often recently, would be repeated in my own country? Twenty-four hours ago, on 14 December, in an interview with *Le Figaro*, I had maintained the contrary: that the Albanian nation, giving the lie to the prophets of doom, would now give proof of its high level of civilization. And now look. Within twenty-four hours violence has broken out. The shadow of doubt weighs upon my conscience; had my departure, instead of accelerating democratization, simply poured oil on the fire?

How to calm the anger of the Albanians? What can you do for them? Celebrate mass, as in Shkodra a month ago? Pull down the statues of Stalin and Lenin? Make speeches? Make promises?

In many respects it is already too late. The lights have dimmed, the play will begin.

Can I say that the half-century of my life coincided in some way with the life of the Albanian people, and that beyond the dictatorship of the proletariat, values have been created which cannot be disputed, and that do honour to the nation? Can I say that it is neither an alibi nor a justification of evil, but a genuine patrimony, as are all tragic truths, and that wanting to cover the world and all it holds with mud is an attempt to show that this people is moribund and immature, as its enemies claim, since after two thousand years and more it took only forty years to degrade it so? To exhort them to be calm, if not for the sake of others, then, at least for love of Kosovo who has just asked that of them, whose message they have heard on radio broadcasts by its most illustrious children, people like R. Qosja and I. Rugova? Can I say that it hasn't been easy for his successor to rid himself of the Enver Hoxha complex, of his legacy, of that heavy anchor? Can I explain that, unlike the true Gorbachev, separated by five successors from the horrible Stalin, the Albanian Gorbachev, Ramiz Alia, came just after Enver Hoxha, so that when showing the face of Gorbachev he was also constrained to show the masks of Malenkov, Khrushchev, Brezhnev, Andropov and Chernenko? Can I remind them that under such circumstances the mantle of the presidency that he inherited had not been made to measure for him, and that Ramiz Alia found himself unprepared, in a tragic arena that required tragic players, on the model of the ancient gladiators?

It is always difficult for an outraged people to lend an ear and listen calmly. They do not want to hear talk of values which they themselves created, since they want only, at that moment, to renounce them. They do not want to hear about the errors they themselves committed, about their long docility, about Ramiz Alia's mantle, or even less about Enver Hoxha, from whose statue they had just broken an arm. There are many things they don't care to hear about, and how understandable that is! But if they are deaf to the message from Kosovo, from that half of the nation that lives on the other side of the border, nothing would be so grievous; it would be their first serious error. In that case justice might desert them. And we know that where justice ends, criminality begins.

Exit. Exit. Exit. *Tiex. Xiet. Itex.* Where is the way out? Where is the right road?

Discord and mutual misunderstanding can spell disaster. The old men of the Balkans say, 'Cry, answer my cry!' But when times change, at the very moment when understanding and agreement are more important than ever, those things are not to be found. Everyone likes to hear his own opinion, his own cry. The people rose in the name of competing values, tolerance, dialogue, pluralism; now they're the first to offend those values. They rush to pull down the busts of Lenin, not thinking that if the statue were anything like the original (as the ancients believed), its eyes would sparkle with pleasure: You want to pull me down, but it was I who pulled you down. The cruelty that I taught you is still with you. And that means that I am still with you, immortal, just as you've been saying yourselves for a hundred years.

It really is the moment of truth for the nation. A time that can certainly be called historic.

Twenty-two years ago, when I thought the socialist world would last for ever, I wrote a poem that I called *Epilogue*. It never occurred to me that the day would come when I would speak of incomprehension and incommunicability among human beings, and certainly not of pardon, guilt and repentance. Yet, if these ideas were not to be found in my intellect or my judgement, I had kept them, it seems, somewhere in the depths of my conscience. It was literature that first awakened them, and, as I wrote at the beginning of these notes, it was literature that led me to freedom.

Here is an extract from that *Epilogue*, dedicated 'to the generations to come,' and published in 1967.

> *You will come in times more tranquil.*
> *Many of our words will have lost all meaning for you,*

Hope

For life will have made many things disappear
Just as perhaps life made the tigers disappear.

Penetrating the powerful ruins
And the majesty of our poems
With your cold logic,
You may try perhaps to judge us.

The ruins will be silent. Only, in return,
Will come the echo of your voices . . .

The poem continues with the drama of incomprehension between the two camps: those who judge, and the ruins that refuse to accept their verdict, because the censors forget 'the tigers who have disappeared'. (It's easy for you to judge, now that the tiger's cries are silenced!)

Exit . . . Repentance, pardon, the remission of sins. Perhaps these are the passages leading out. Half the nation, on the far bank, has given us another message: the remission of vengeance. It resembled an act taken from an ancient tragedy, but it's worthy of a place among the most modern political acts.

The Albanian nation, banished from Europe for so many years, knocks again, like the prodigal son, at its gate. In its hand it bears new badges and new banners. Albania means to prove that it does not forget, but it does pardon.

The nation takes upon itself its share of blame, and distributes it among its people. That is the only precept of the dictatorship that it holds to, but it reshapes it according to its own conception. It does this not to preserve the dictatorship, but to bury it together with the serpent's eggs that the dictatorship had hoped to palm off on the nation.

The first poem in the literature of Albania was written and published in 1592 by Lek Matrenga, poet and priest. It is entitled *Dirge*, and begins with this verse:

Albanian Spring

For all I pray who seek pardon
Good Christians, men and women
That in the name of our Lord you find mercy
For among us there is none without sin.

Perhaps it is not by chance that the first words in our literature are a plea for pardon. Perhaps it is a sign of Providence.

France, December 1990

Notes

Introduction

1.   Published in Albania in 1990. A translated version appeared in France in the autumn of 1991.

2.   Published in Albania in 1981 under the title *Nepunesi i pallatit te endrrave*. First French-language edition published in France in 1990 by Librairie Arthème Fayard. First English-language edition published in Britain in 1993 by Harvill, an imprint of Harper Collins Publishers.

Part One

1.   At the time these pages were written, in November 1990, no one could foresee what was to happen one month later. In December, when this book was at press, one day after demonstrations by students and intellectuals, democracy had succeeded in forging ahead in Albania. Thus, after the sentence, 'That kind of spring generally takes root in winter,' one might well add, 'In winter, too, the crop is gathered.'

2.   T. Lubonja, Director of the Albanian Radio and Television Network. He was convicted by the famous Fourth Plenary Session in 1973. He is mentioned in all the manuals, doctoral theses, and speeches in the *History of the P.T.A.*, as head of the phantom group, 'T. Lubonja–F. Paçrami' (or the cultural conspiracy which inaugurated the wave of convictions from 1973 to 1976).

3.   Called *The Red Pashas* only later by the public. This poem of a hundred verses was sent to the printer by the Deputy Editor-in-Chief of the journal *Drita (The Light)*. On a Saturday night (the journal appeared every Sunday), under circumstances which are still obscure, one copy reached the home of Hysni Kapo, and another that of Enver Hoxha. The poem was censured immediately. I had to return all copies plus the manuscript to the secretary of the Writers' Union, A.K.; thus the text was lost, or perhaps is to be found in the archives of the Central Committee.

I can remember only the first line, 'The Politburo met this afternoon,' and then the following stanza:

Red Pashas, barons with a Party card,
Oil magnates, beys and thieves,
Singing old liturgical hymns
You lead the coffin of the revolution to its grave.

Years later, the writer, L. Siliqi, who had attended the meeting in Ramiz Alia's office, said to me: 'Yesterday, I found the notes that I took during that meeting. I couldn't believe my eyes. I don't think that any writer has been criticized more savagely in all of the socialist countries.'

4.   In his study, Pipa tried to show that through my novels *The Drums of Rain*, *The Great Winter*, and especially *Chronicle in Stone*, I had opposed the communist regime, and particularly, Enver Hoxha. Pipa's accusations, most serious in the case of *Chronicle in Stone*, were enough to put me in prison for life, or worse. Pipa knew quite well that a number of people had been liquidated for matters having to do with the private life of Enver Hoxha.

5.   The Sigurimi wanted to avenge itself on Dr Ylli Popa when that law was rejected. A long campaign of denigration was unleashed upon him. Trained to seize every possible opportunity, the Sigurimi exploited the fact that Popa had been one of Enver Hoxha's physicians. The accusation was made in two opposing directions: in restricted circles they announced that the doctor, who had liberal views and who had taken part in many international gatherings, had shortened the life of Enver Hoxha. In larger circles, they said something very different, spreading rumours that Popa, as Enver Hoxha's physician, had been the beneficiary of special privileges. As a result, the doctor was spurned by both sides.

The truth is that besides his skill as a physician, Dr Popa was an eminent intellectual. He made several journeys abroad because of his talents and quite exceptional cultivation, and brought honour to Albanian science. As for his having been a member of the team of doctors treating Enver Hoxha, I believe that beyond the difficulties and the anxiety he had to endure because of that post, there is nothing to be said. While this book was at press [the 1991 Albanian edition—*Editor's note*], Dr Popa was appointed to the Committee for the Defence of Human Rights, established in Tirana on 22 December 1990.

6.   Foto Çami was the only member of the Politburo to hold the title 'academician'. As might be expected, he was soon identified as liberal and reformist in his views. At one time he had been regarded as the second-in-command of the Albanian state, but he lost influence. The praise given him by the foreign press seemed to be the primary reason for his decline. The appointment of Xhelil Gjoni, after the events took place in July, brought about his fall. Çami's recent exclusion from the Politburo, along with other reactionaries who were generally abhorred, seemed most disconcerting and illogical. It's not impossible that this measure was taken simply to disorient the public, or to provide compensation in the regime's new game of 'balance'. It's also possible that, shocked by the brutality with which certain students had been treated a few days earlier (something he had expressed on other occasions when the use of violence was suggested), he had simply handed in his resignation.

7.   It would seem that my expectations were correct. The fact that students and intellectuals became, for the first time, widely engaged in the struggle for democracy confirms that my departure was not a source of further discouragement, as some believed, but quite the contrary. According to the coverage in the press, the shock struck home. That has been confirmed in dozens of letters sent to me from Albania. Indeed, the appearance on the scene of the intelligentsia, in December 1990, was decisive in advancing democracy. Several days after I left Albania, the regime permitted the sale of my two latest books, previously kept out of circulation. In a few hours nearly all copies had been sold. But there was something more important: it was the first time the Albanian government had shown a hitherto unknown tolerance; books written by an exile were allowed on the market (no East European government had ever permitted this)—and only forty-eight hours after his departure. It demonstrated that, for the first time in half a century, the regime was willing to live with a member of the opposition. For all intents and purposes, it was a tacit acceptance of the democratic movement. The Albanian intelligentsia, students in the lead, had seized the day.

8.   The Albanian edition was published just before the author's departure in 1990.

9.   *Invitation to the Writer's Studio* was published in France as *Invitation à l'atelier* in autumn 1991; *The Monster* was also published in

autumn 1991 as *Le Monstre; The Pyramid of Cheops* was published as *La Pyramide de Khéops* in 1992.

10. From this group of intellectuals the founders of the Democratic Party, the first opposition party in Albania, were to emerge. Included in that group were notably Dr Berisha and Dr Pashko, plus the well-known writer and journalist S. Mustafaj, among others. According to several sources, Dr Berisha saw the President at his home in order to present the claims of his students, and he was promised that the opposition would be authorized to pursue its aims. A few days later, Berisha and Pashko asked the Prime Minister to officially recognize their party. They succeeded in their mission, and the party, thus recognized both inside Albania and abroad, has since engaged itself in the difficult struggle for democracy.

Contrary to what people expected, Albania was the first communist country to authorize, within hours of recognizing the right to pluralistic representation, the existence of a credible opposition party, one with a clear programme that was both worthy and culturally rich.

(Another party, claimed to have been formed earlier (and illegally) as the Ecologists' Party, and in whose programme there is no discernible evidence of opposition, rather reminds me of the clandestine communist 'Submarines' in 1945!)

11. During the embassy crisis, many well-known people in the cultural world were asked to make statements condemning the refugees. Some accepted, others did not. Though I had categorically refused and made no declaration whatsoever, the Sigurimi, benefiting from its prior experience in discrediting people, circulated a rumour to the contrary. Unfortunately, it was successful in spreading the falsehood. Its staff leaked the rumour to foreign journalists, some of whom, without bothering to verify the claim, then circulated this lie perpetrated by the Albanian Sigurimi.

That deception had the particular aim of maligning me before that fraction of the population whose relatives had left the country. The same procedure was used, though in a smaller circle, with respect to my book *Invitation to the Writer's Studio*, although that time the aim was to malign me before my colleagues. The rumour claimed that the French translation of my book—not yet published at the time!—contained attacks directed against certain Albanian writers. The Sigurimi imagined it would be easy to persuade them to make statements against me. But the Sigurimi's failure was complete. There were a few exceptions—the poet R. Marku, the painter Z. Mati, A. Kondo, and some people unknown to me who presented themselves to foreign journalists as men of letters—but genuine writers and artists refused to believe the Stalinists.

Part Two

1. Though he described himself as a friend of democracy, whenever something happened in Albania that might quicken hope, A. Pipa promptly began discouraging people. When in December 1990, contrary to his prophecies, the first opposition party was actually established, he was one of the rare Albanians to make pronouncements against it. The first democratic party and its founders were attacked equally by hostile forces like the Albanian Sigurimi and by the most confirmed reactionaries.

2. Zylyftar Ramizi, Chief of National Security. He was discharged from office four months after that letter was written.

3. Spiro Koleka, long-time member of the Politburo and Vice-Prime Minister, later Vice-President of the Presidium of the People's Assembly. He played an important role in Albania's economic ruin.

4. At the time I wrote this letter, Rita Marko was a member of the Politburo. He lost that post after the events of July.

5. Kadri Hazbiu, member of the Politburo and Minister of the Interior. He played a central role in eliminating the ex-Prime Minister, M. Shehu, in 1981. He was condemned to death and shot in 1982. It was Feçor Shehu who replaced Hazbiu as Minister of the Interior. He, too, was condemned to death and shot, like his predecessor, in 1982.

6. Extracts from that interview were published in the newspaper *Le Monde*.

7. It was my novel *Chronicle in Stone* that A. Pipa referred to and about which he offered a monstrous interpretation that might very well have earned me a death sentence. The President must be aware of that interpretation since he was Chief of Propaganda at the time. It's possible that he forbore to transmit the information to Enver Hoxha.

Part Three

1. To prove the contrary, the communists were obliged to institute an exemplary puritanism among the partisans. It was so severe that it

caused tragic situations. Dozens of partisans, boys and girls, were shot because of love affairs. People remember the execution of the beautiful R. Gjebrea, who had fallen in love with the war hero, Z. Koka. Her fiancé, N. Spiru, one of the directors of the movement, spoke out against her execution. If Z. Koka himself was not condemned, it's probably because he was believed to be innocent. But in the first battle thereafter, he rushed at the German machine-guns and was riddled with bullets. Afterwards a song was composed about the story. To complete the circle, the third actor in the tragedy, N. Spiru, committed suicide in 1948 for political reasons.

There is also a dramatic story of the murders committed by Sheh Karbunara of two high-ranking members of the clergy in 1945 because of a love affair. At that time love relations were permitted by the communists, but they were still forbidden by religion.

2. The clandestine character of the Party and its members brought about in those years a most significant form of trauma. Many partisans who'd been involved in the fighting imagined that they were all equal. In the years 1944–1945 they first came to understand that a fraction of them, carefully selected, were communists. The worst of it was that the elite hung back in the shadows, just as they had earlier, during the occupation. The bitterness was immense when these things became clear, particularly among the idealistic partisans.

3. Purposely or not, certain Western countries contributed to Albania's isolationism. Instead of acting so as not to abandon Albania, they turned their backs on the communist regime; in effect, however, they were really turning their backs on the Albanian people. In doing so, they only fulfilled the wishes of the communist state.

The Italian position is a fair sample of that attitude. Going against an old tradition of friendship.between the two countries, dating back to the Middle Ages, contemporary Italy has carried out a policy of continual hostility towards Albania. It tried to occupy the country in 1920, and succeeded on 7 April 1939. Italy has never apologized to Albania for its incursions, most notably for the fascist invasion. That invasion was at the heart of Albania's troubles, because it ultimately led to Albania's attachment once more to the East. While Italy has sent delegations to various Ukrainian villages to thank them for having protected small groups of five or six Italian soldiers, and has also built commemorative monuments there, it has never shown the least gratitude to the Albanian people for the care they had taken of whole armies, of tens of thousands of Italian soldiers who remained in Albania in 1943 after the capitulation of their own country. Even though they were enemies yesterday, at the mercy of the Albanians, no vengeance was carried out upon those soldiers, and they were even lodged and protected at a time when the Nazis were searching for them to take reprisals. Nothing can justify the Italian attitude. It is true that the Albanians did not hold the Italian soldiers in great esteem but called them *pepino* or *goiters*, nevertheless, when those Italian soldiers fell into their hands their clemency was unequalled. Neither did the Albanian contempt for the Italian soldiers keep them from respecting Italian culture. As a matter of fact, it is among the Italians that there is bad feeling and a desire to take revenge for the way the Albanians condescended to them. After the installation of the communist regime in Albania, official Italy acted as if Albania did not exist. Her name was almost never mentioned, not even in the weather bulletins, despite the fact that Albania is a mere hundred kilometres from Italy, and the clouds do occasionally go there or turn in her direction.

Such an attitude on radio broadcasts and on Italian television is simply unpardonable. Knowing very well that it is being watched day and night in Albania, Italy has done almost nothing to help speed the process of democratization at the end of this decade. Its silence in fact used to help the totalitarian state, which worked long years to assure it.

4.   A bomb thrown at the Soviet embassy by the Albanian Sigurimi, on the advice of the Soviets, served as a pretext for strengthening 'the class struggle,' which is to say, for spreading terror. The Minister of Justice refused to endorse the sentences meted out with no trial for the persons arrested on that occasion.

5.   Although several decades had passed, criticizing *Koçixoxism* in literature was nearly impossible. In 1973 the Minister of the Interior, Kadri Hazbiu, attempted to officially ban my novel *The Great Winter* because the book mentioned the crimes of Koçi Xoxe.

6.   Fan Noli had lived in the United States, where he died in 1962. Throughout his life, though it might have been expected, he almost never attacked the communists. Apparently, the unresolved national questions (our dangerous neighbours, but especially the question of Kosovo) dissuaded him from speaking of it. At his death, when one might have hoped that he had left behind something useful on the subject, there was nothing. For the same reasons, perhaps, he may have thought that his

work would be banned on the pretext of some declaration on his part, which would be much more damaging to Albanian culture than would the absence of any such declaration.

Lasgush Poradeci died in Tirana in 1988. He was not a partisan of the regime, but he never wrote anything against it. People expected to find certain things after his death, but that expectation has not yet been fulfilled, and it appears that there is nothing to hope for in that way. It is probable that if he had in fact left manuscripts, they could very well have fallen into the hands of the Sigurimi, since a portion of his archives was stolen after his death.

7.   A letter written to *Le Monde* about me, by Nils Anderson, a Swede, dealt with that issue together with other observations. What Anderson did not say was that he has been and still is the translator, publisher, and propagandist of the works of Enver Hoxha in a number of countries. That explains his position with regard to the development of democracy in Albania. The friendship of Marxist-Leninists like Nils Anderson has cost Albania dear, for it is based upon a disaster, Albania's isolation and its hostility to the rest of the world. In a democratic Albania those Marxist friends would lose their monopoly and the privilege that they have enjoyed in that country, so it's understandable that they are opponents of democracy. In his letter, Nils Anderson mentions the interesting fact that in 1973, when my novel, *The Great Writer*, was under attack, it was really aimed at Ramiz Alia. (Nils Anderson was very close to the Albanian leaders, and his private knowledge of them is by no means insignificant.) Though it is certain that at the time in question Ramiz Alia was a target, Anderson is simply not credible when he claims that Enver Hoxha himself was in the line of fire. It is as if one were to say that Stalin was threatened in the Soviet Union by the conservatives because he was too liberal!

8.   People went to unbelievable lengths to avoid that entrapment. My good friend, the poet and critic D. Siliqi, told me that in 1961 he managed to escape the tentacles of the Sigurimi. Its agents met D. Siliqi, and, employing one of their classic methods, a 'clean one', they asked him to collaborate with them in the name of communism, etc. Siliqi refused.

They tried again with another classic method (not 'clean' this time): they reminded him of certain private letters that he had written. At a loss for an answer, Siliqi told them that he would think it over. At the next meeting of the Party, when they had got to 'other business', he rose to ask for the floor. He took the floor, and to the astonishment of all those present, he declared, 'A few days ago, the comrades from the Sigurimi suggested that I become a spy. Before giving them my answer, I would like to know what the comrades of this organization think about the matter.'

The Party Secretary turned red, and then yellow. 'What's the meaning of this, Comrade? We're not here to discuss anything like that!'

'And why not?' Siliqi said. 'We are here among the Party, and no one may conceal things from the Party; don't you agree?'

Thereafter they left Siliqi in peace.

9. Discrediting illustrious persons is a permanent objective of communist dictatorship. It's generally carried out in two areas, the past and the present. Marxist slogans like, 'It is the masses that shape history,' 'Let us take a dialectical position towards the past,' etc, serve as scientific justification for denigrating the grand figures of history. At school, they never forget to emphasize their 'mistakes', their 'ideological failing', including the poets of the nation like N. Frashëri. The attempts made by Enver Hoxha to discredit Fan Noli on the eve of his centenary are most significant. Those views have not spared Gjergj Kastrioti (Skanderberg). Given that he was the national hero, defender of Christianity against Islam, the man who upheld Albania's connection with Western Europe, it was to be expected that there would be no common ground with the communists. In the period from 1946 to 1948, under pressure from the Yugoslavs, he was not to be mentioned except to be denigrated. In 1967, his fifth centennial was celebrated in Albania in the most lukewarm manner, and emphasis was placed on the thesis that 'Albanian history must be focused further on the role of the masses in history, and should not exaggerate the role of the princes of the Middle Ages.'

The clash in the shadows between Gjergj Kastrioti and Enver Hoxha was inevitable.

When, in April 1985, Enver Hoxha was described in his funeral speech as 'the most illustrious man in all of Albania's history', that was not a chance expression—it had taken years of effort to establish. In order to be the most illustrious figure of the nation, they had to dethrone the holder of the title for half a millennium: Skanderberg. The first battle in daylight between Kastrioti and Hoxha took place in Paris, in the Place de la Villette, when that square was baptized in the name of Skanderberg. The Albanian government, not content with simply failing to show gratitude to France for paying homage to its national hero, not only boycotted the inaugural ceremony as well as the high mass celebrated in Notre Dame, but also intervened with the mayor of Paris, Jacques Chirac, to stop the ceremony. The government's annoyance showed clearly in its belief that the first Albanian name to grace a square in Paris should have been that of Enver Hoxha, and no one else. At La Villette in Paris the medieval prince overcame the First Secretary of the Workers' Party of Albania. But the final assault took place in Tirana, in Skanderberg Square, no less, where the two statues confronted each other. The small minds of the leaders and of the sculptors, S. Haderi and S. Shijaku, who insisted on erecting the statue of Enver Hoxha in a square that bore another name (a very rare thing that tends to suggest that in order to take revenge for what had occurred in Paris, the communists were thinking that perhaps some day the prince would be expelled from the square) could only go counter to the goal they sought.

Nor was there any less ardour to discredit living persons. The meeting with President Ramiz Alia and the intellectuals in August 1990 in Tirana was one of the last examples of that fever. After that meeting, everything possible was done to throw mud at the intellectuals, to create distrust between them and the people. The mystification spread everywhere by the Sigurimi was this: Ramiz Alia had asked the intellectuals if they favoured a multi-party system, and they were too cowardly to say yes.

While the stenographic record of that meeting is hidden away in a 'top secret' file, it is not an exact transcription of what had occurred. Not only are important sentences and remarks missing from the account, but it does not give a trace of the atmosphere of the encounter. The truth is very different from the message broadcast all over the country by agents of the Sigurimi, assisted at times by certain foreign journalists. The meeting opened in an unpleasant mood. No one knew why we had been summoned, nor who the other participants were. One among us, M.P., having looked about him and seen that many of us were intellectuals whose names appeared on the 'Sigurimi lists', said in a low voice, 'Let me know if you're certain that we'll all get out of here in one piece!'

The arrival of Ramiz Alia, not accompanied by Foto Çami but by Xhelil Gjoni, 'the strong man' whom the intellectuals were not happy with, cast further gloom on the meeting. The chance of a deliberate provocation seemed plausible. The speech delivered by Ramiz Alia was harsh and showed no sign of any desire for dialogue; it was a threat rather than a speech. But the intellectuals faced up to it.

The first question that the President was asked was about police violence, and the persons who had disappeared in the Mountain of Caves. That question and others of the same sort led to a radical change of tone, and the President adopted a defensive stance.

The discussion about multi-party politics, while brief, was the most delicate issue of the meeting. It began after a recess, at about two o'clock in the afternoon. Despite the President's virulent attack on 'that Trojan horse', we were resolved to demand plural parties. G. Pashko, who sat beside me, said to me in a low voice, 'I'm getting up; now it's my turn to talk to him about it.'

I told him, 'It's probably better that I do that, because it is harder for him to be angry with me.' I was preparing my first sentence—the devil isn't as black as he's painted—when Ramiz Alia, before letting us speak, said to Dr Berisha and to me (we were sitting side by side), 'Before you speak, I want to tell you this: according to documents in my possession, it is clear that international reactionaries are trying to use plural parties to overthrow by violence the government of the people of Albania. Tell me if you yourselves are in agreement about it. Tell me, Berisha, do you agree about delivering the Party to them?'

S. Berisha, to whom the President had said harsh things two or three times in his meeting, found himself in a difficult situation.

He answered in more or less these terms: Naturally, that is not what I want. However, one must never say, *never more*.

'And you?' said the President, turning to me.

These are the exchanges after that:

I. K.: 'I do not know how that squares with the legal view.'

R. A.: 'You don't know? If someone else told me that, I would believe it, but you?'

I. K.: 'I don't know how to take up this matter here. Whatever it does mean, all this discussion is too heavy with political assumptions.'

The academician, L. Omari, broke in to suggest a more acceptable formula for foreign relations.

That was the debate over party pluralism. I have not managed to consult the 'confidential register', but reliable sources have told me that without doubt that was the only part of the meeting to have been transcribed inaccurately.

I still hold the conviction that the most that might have been said there was in fact said. Nearly the whole of the future opposition was present at that meeting, and there was deliberate provocation designed to give those in opposition a preventive shock that would eliminate them from the field, and that state is likely to prevail for some time.

10. The true reasons for the blow were learned only later and only in certain cases, but in general they remained mysterious. While one might imagine, for example, that the reason for Todi Lubonja's fall was his reputation as a liberal, and even more because of his friendship with Ramiz Alia, whose elimination was of great interest to the powerful clans of Hysni Kapo and M. Shelhu, one may not ignore the fact that Paçrami's passion as a dramatist was not condoned. 'Instead of writing three-act plays, you would do better to take note of the play of thirty thousand acts written by the people.' These words were spoken by Enver Hoxha in a meeting that was the prelude to the fall of that playwright.

It has not been possible up to the present time to find the motive behind the blow that struck the military. They began by condemning the minister, B. Balluku, while two of his aides, P. Dume and H. Çako, who had opposed him for years (as everyone knew), were promoted, as was generally expected. However, some months later, Dume and Çako too were arrested; it was claimed that their so-called 'hostility' was nothing but 'a smoke-screen' behind which they lied to the Party and covered the traces of their 'plot'. All three were shot at the same time.

As for the group of economists, one can understand the causes which led to the condemning of K. Theodosi, who had been in France with Enver Hoxha when they were young, and of A. Kellezi, Theodosi's friend. But no one has ever explained the condemning of K. Ngjela and V. Kati, Minister and Vice-Minister of Commerce. Similarly, the real motive behind the condemning of the petroleum engineers is a mystery.

While it is understandable that M. Shehu and Kadri Hazbiu were eliminated, the case of the Minister of Foreign Affairs, N. Nase, of the Minister of Health, M. Ziçishti, and a dozen others also involved in the last trials of 1981–1982, remain a mystery.

11. The Fourth Plenary Session, of unhappy memory, has served for a long time as a scarecrow with which to threaten the intellectuals in general, and the writers and artists in particular: we must forget the

lessons of the Fourth Plenary Session. Do you remember how the Fourth Plenary Session ended? It will return, the Fourth Plenary Session!

12. Spiro Koleka, who was in charge of the economy and of construction for a long time, is particularly famous for having diminished the size of living accommodation. By interpreting communist doctrine according to his own narrow vision, he became a genuine plague for the Albanian people, who had traditionally lived in large houses.

13. Words spoken by Spiro Koleka to the architect P. Kolevica, who was accused several times of being a bourgeois and a revisionist, simply because he had tried to design buildings which had, among other things, the advantage of elegance.

14. The story of that Club is significant. Next to the National Theatre and facing the Ministry of the Interior, it was a thorn in the side of the Sigurimi. (What is that Petöfi Club? We ought to close down that lair of counter-revolutionaries.)

The demand to abolish it was not accepted, so the Club did not close. But they managed to get rid of it in a more insidious fashion. An exhibition about Cambodia was set up on the premises. People came every day to ask when the Club would be open again. The writers flocked there, and the actors of the National Theatre, all looking dismayed. But the exhibition went on for eight months.

When the Club did open, it was unrecognizable. It was as if Cambodia had made a desert of it. Nobody had the heart to laugh again; all of its old lively character was gone.

The Club, that place of pleasant encounters and discussions after dinner, that place where it was so nice to dance, was completely disfigured. Now there was one meeting after another. Some of these were violent, most painful. Nevertheless, from time to time it remembered its youthful gaiety, for example, on the occasion of the splendid scandal provoked by Professor S. Luarasi, who defended my novel, *The General of the Dead Army*, about which the critics had gone off like a rocket. That scandal was the last one, and Professor Luarasi, a distinguished Germanist, translator of Goethe and Schiller, found himself banned from the Club.

15. What we call dual personality is not always a terrible thing. It came about with the passing of time, one part of the person continuing to advance while the other remained in place. Writers of middling worth or limited talent, who might have served Stalinism zealously, refrained,

and what is more, often distinguished themselves because of their human qualities. Though he had been Party Secretary of the Writers' Union, the playwright I. Uruçi stood out because of his manners and his integrity. His being convicted and imprisoned was one of those shots in the dark that were typical of that time. In prison, he had never understood the reason for his incarceration (indeed, that has always been a mystery for everyone); being the idealist that he was, he kept his faith in communism to the end of his life. In the case of other writers such as N. Bulka, L. Siliqi, S. Spasse, etc, something quite astonishing happened. Their creative powers waned, worn out like an engine that turns against the force of the brake, and by sheer inertia produced works that were in every sense obsolete.

Despite that, it did not prevent them from being decent and upright; far from constituting an obstacle to progress, they were at pains to help the cause as much as they could. This form of 'doubling,' connected in some cases with the anti-fascist movement (I. Uruçi, L. Siliqi, Andoni, etc), was more related to the suppression of their experience of evil, which I have mentioned above, than to a split personality. Other writers, such as Dhori Qiriazi, a talented poet, kept away from the agitation of that era; but their probity, since it was passive in this regard, did not play much of a role in the emancipation of literature. Faced by this dilemma, namely either to pay for going down into that arena of sound and fury, or to make no such sacrifice and to shrink into themselves, half forgotten, they had chosen the latter course.

In all domains of life, just as was happening in the realm of literature, people resisted the evil. In the ranks of the communists, thousands of respectable people tried, when they could and how they could, to do something for their country. At the start of the 1960s, the Writers' Club was a mere fragment of the mosaic of life. There were dozens of similar institutions. I never lost sight of that when, in an interview with David Binder, published in *The New York Times* in November of 1990, I declared that I had no intention to throw mud at a half-century of the life of my fellow Albanians. During that time there were various periods in which the worst troubles were in retreat on every front. The period from 1958 to 1961 is remembered for that. So are the years from 1969 to 1971. It was during that time that in a meeting with A. Mero, then First Secretary of the Youth Movement, Enver Hoxha declared that the people who did not love our young men and women ought to resign their posts.

One week later, at a meeting of the Secretariat of the Central Committee, to which a number of young people had been invited, after learning that some of them spoke English and French, Enver Hoxha astounded the other Party chiefs by asking the young people to speak in those tongues. After hearing them, he said, 'From now on, the speaking of English or French in the Politburo of the Workers' Party of Albania should surprise no one.'

This sign and other similar ones made it possible to hope that Enver Hoxha was preparing to make overtures to Europe. Everyone expected that feverishly. But meanwhile the Ministry of the Interior, goaded it seems by the most hardened Stalinists like Kadri Hazbiu and Hysni Kapo, were cooking up a report showing that if Enver Hoxha were to make the fatal mistake of opening our country to the West, it would bring about his downfall. As is well known, that tendency prevailed in 1973, which was a tragedy for Albania.

16. To go against Marx's formula by arguing that 'The true meaning of life is not struggle but life itself,' as G. Sorman stressed, would make you a declared enemy of the revolution. As for dynamism, which was endlessly praised, it would be hard to find a better example than Genghis Khan. It's not by chance that during the Cultural Revolution in China, Mao Zedong referred a number of times, and sympathetically, to that desert nomad.

17. In the middle of the 1970s, on the eve of the closing of the country to the rest of the world, dozens of labourers were hired to take up posts in the Ministry of Foreign Affairs and the Ministry of Foreign Commerce. They called it 'the renewal of institutions by the working class'. The naive were surprised ('How can they carry out foreign policy and foreign commerce?' they asked. 'Those people are quite ignorant, they don't understand foreign languages.') They were scandalized, they sent letters to 'higher authority' because they did not understand that the government had a particular goal in sight: to reduce to zero the few surviving links with foreign nations. The appointment as Minister of Commerce of a certain Nedin Hoxha, known for being obtuse and stubborn, was significant in itself.

18. Another example of Sofo Lazri's conduct, what one might call an everyday misrepresentation. It concerns the publication abroad of *Megjeni*, to which he was hostile at first. 'Listen,' he said in the course of our conversation, 'I've seen a report from our ambassador in Paris that

mentions your friend Jacques Attala.' 'Jacques Attali,' I said.

'It comes to the same thing. Since you have made his acquaintance, the ambassador thinks that he might be able to help the development of our relations with France. Personally, I don't believe it for a minute, because that Jacques Attali, as I have verified from other sources, is responsible only for literature, and he has no influence whatever with the government.' 'That's absolutely false,' I replied. 'You may know lots of things, but here you are absolutely wrong. Jacques Attali is special adviser to President Mitterrand, and his influence is equal to that of the cabinet ministers.' 'That makes no difference. You have your position, I have mine,' he said, ending our conversation. It is clear, given his intractable character, that he was stubbornly opposing any *rapprochement* with France, and that he did all he could to break every tie with that country.

Sheer lies of that sort are particularly noxious when they deal with history. A serious misrepresentation of history must excite grief and rage. Many historians have dishonoured themselves for ever in espousing monstrous falsifications on subjects like Albanian-Russian relations. From being a ferocious enemy of the Albanian government and people, as she had always been because of her preference for the Serbs and the Montenegrins, Russia had been transformed into a pretended friend. The contrary thing has happened with Western countries, who are all accused of being hostile to Albania. This denaturing of history, to give aid and comfort to the policy of the day, is one of the blackest pages of the culture of Albania in this century.

But they have not stopped there. They also emphasized the fictitious sympathy of Lenin for Albania—purely imaginary. They also stressed Stalin's pretended sympathy, and they hid the truth: his hatred of Albania and his insults to the nation.

People also remember the manipulations to which our history was subject. Enver Hoxha himself wrote an essay on the revolt of Haxhi Qamili, describing it as a peasant rebellion against the feudal order, while everyone knows that is was nothing more than a pro-Turkish movement that openly sought to split Albania from Europe and to reunite it with Turkey. While praising to the skies an obscure Haxhi Qamili, they busied themselves with tarnishing the reputation of great figures like the founder of the first Albanian state, Ismail Qemal. And they heaped abuse on others. Some were described as agents of Western powers; others were deplored for extravagant 'weaknesses'; in other cases still, they simply lied. For example, F. Konica was rooted out of the pages of Albanian literature on the pretext that he had been King Zog's ambassador to the United States, forgetting that at the very same time Enver Hoxha had been in the King's consular service. In order to incriminate Gjergj Fishta, they resorted to another bit of low cunning: his satirical poem, *Let the World Know that Gjergj is No Longer Albanian*, in the verses of which he mocks those people who accused him of being unpatriotic, was presented as an actual declaration by the poet. The same trick was used in the case of the novel *Flag Merchants*, by Ernest Koliqi, based on the title alone so as to claim that the author had admitted that he had been a seller of flags. (The novel had been written expressly to stigmatize flag merchants and flag wavers.)

The mechanics of the grand hoax, the creation of the lacunae and blank spaces in history texts, including techniques ranging from the disappearance of names and facts to the retouching of photographs in which the heads of the departed fell as easily as they had fallen in life itself. The central archives of the government, including those of the Party, were subject to periodic visitations; expunging compromising clues was the obsession of the communist dictators. That meant the destruction of documents and entire files, and went as far as the disappearance of the bodies of condemned people, to ensure that in future there would not be the slightest impulse to make a pilgrimage to the tombs of the dead. The same reason prompted the destruction of commemorative plaques and the annihilation of various kinds of evidence, like the demolition of houses in which people chastised by the government had lived. The latest example was the demolition of the house of Dr Papavrami in 1986, when his grandson, Tedi Papavrami, a well-known violinist, had fled to France.

19. Here is how things happen. Comrade X is going to visit Vienna, for medical reasons. In most such cases he would be accompanied by one or other member of his family, his daughter, his son-in-law, his daughter-in-law. At that point, communist doctrine has not been breached. The fate of the revolution depends on the health of its directors. As for the son-in-law and daughter-in-law, it might seem at first that principle has been wounded, but if we look at it carefully, taking into account the opinion of the doctors that the moral comfort of Comrade X would hasten his recovery, the presence of the son-in-law or

daughter-in-law is justified. Up to this point, then, Marxism-Leninism has been respected. However, then comes the moment (the fatal moment) when Comrade X, or more frequently his wife or his daughter-in-law, wants to visit the shops in Vienna. Obviously, that takes money. The rules of a small, thrifty country forbid the expense. Well, what can be done? There is a danger that the desperation of the wife or the daughter-in-law of Comrade X might have unpleasant repercussions upon his health. Yet this does not constitute a convincing argument. It is just at this point that the immortal proletarian doctrine once again offers salvation. The principle of vigilance towards the class enemy, particularly in the West, saves the situation. The enemy must never know with any precision what Comrade X's illness is, nor the visitors he receives, the medicines he buys, etc. For that reason, so as not to abandon any document to the class enemy, all the bills, the physician's charges, the pharmaceutical expenses, these must be destroyed. And that is exactly what happens. They disappear, and are replaced by a few figures scribbled on a pad. One can easily imagine that those figures would not stand up to serious scrutiny.

20. Those brutal attacks continued in the press and on television until November of 1990. The latest pretext was the publication of an anonymous letter in *Zeri i Popullit*, which took aim at a broadcast in Albanian by *The Voice of America*, and in particular the journalist and scholar, Elez Biberaj, unjustly described as a traitor, spy, etc, while the persons interviewed were treated as gullible fools. The fools in question were the flower of the intelligentsia of Albania and Kosovo, and those journals, to their shame, allowed a ruffian who did not dare give his name to insult whomever he chose. The very fact of having published anonymous letters in the leading journal of the country was in itself a deeply immoral act. But anonymous letters had been given free reign from the time that Enver Hoxha had shown himself openly in favour of those things. They were perfect for all sorts of hoaxes, in the fog that characterized that world.

21. A year earlier, one of those 'simple' citizens had reprimanded the engineer, Z. M.: 'What do you do, you intellectuals? Why don't you do something?'

'You have the right to express your views,' Z. M. answered. 'But I too have the right to ask you, what do you do?'

'Me? What do I do? I'm just an ordinary man. I'm not like you. If I were, then you'd see something.'

'You mean that you're not famous?' Z. M. said. 'Would you like to be a hero, doesn't it bother you to be ordinary? I'll tell you how to go about it. It will cost almost nothing, just twelve old leks. Buy a litre of gasoline and burn yourself to death in Skanderberg Square, like Jan Palach in Czechoslovakia. I guarantee that you'll be immortal.'

22. I remember a strange episode that happened in 1967. I was in the city of Berat, 'in order to be among the people'. The great textile complex, with its six thousand workers, mostly women and young girls, had just opened. The entire city was revitalized by that factory. There was an economic renaissance, and a moral one as well. Life there was interesting, young engineers who came from all over Albania spent sleepless nights at one another's lodgings, went dancing every weekend, the girls made love, the rhythm of the days had changed.

But one fine day in November there arrived from Tirana G. Çuçi, one of the most sinister figures of that era. For two days he closeted himself with the principal official of the city. On the third day, when I went to the plant, I could not believe my eyes.

It was as if the factory had gone into mourning. The young women bustled about their machines, blushing. Some had tears in their eyes. Someone tore down the poster announcing the dance on the following Saturday.

'What's happened?' I asked one of my engineer friends.

'Don't ask. We had a meeting last night. They accused us of being lukewarm about the class struggle. New directives have come from Tirana. Today, we had meetings in every shop. In some of them, people burst into tears.'

'What directives? Why did they burst into tears?'

'How could you not cry?' he said. 'It was really lamentable. No fraternizing or friendship with people who have any kind of stain on their records. Strengthening the class struggle.'

23. Take the case of Nina F., a Russian woman who had married an Albanian during the period of friendship between the two countries. After the breaking of relations, she had no way of getting news to her family, or sending news to them. She died in Tirana in 1987. At the burial, after her sister-in-law wept for her according to local custom, the representative of the Front in that region spoke: 'We have come here to say a last farewell to Comrade Nina F., member of the Albanian

Democratic Front, a devoted engineer, faithful to the lessons of the Party and of Comrade Enver.' Not a word about her Russian nationality, or of the letters that never reached Moscow, or the suffering that might have aggravated her illness and hastened her death.

24. At the very time when this book is going to press, the wave of violence has quickly been spent in Albania. It is owing to the pressure of the entire population, rather than to the police and the military, that things have quieted down. (Some people have remarked that 'the forces of order' have not only been unperturbed by the situation, but have actually fomented trouble deliberately in a number of cases.) The Albanians, whom I had correctly gauged, have quickly reached a national consensus to create an opposition at once resolute and sophisticated in every sense. The fact that the intellectuals and the students have taken the lead is significant. By the close of 1990, the Albanian Democratic Party has become one of the strongest and most clear-sighted of the opposition parties created in Eastern Europe. By that act, belying cynical prophesies, the Albanians have shown the world that they are more civilized and more European than the people who uttered such prophesies day and night, while turning their backs upon them.

France, December 1990–January 1991